Movelle U

MW01100886

# *Discover* GENESIS
## ABRAHAM AND SARAH

by
Carol Veldman Rudie

FAITH
ALIVE.
Christian Resources

Grand Rapids, Michigan

We thank Carol Veldman Rudie of Minneapolis, Minnesota, for writing this study. We also thank Deb Fennema of Kenosha, Wisconsin, who contributed to this revision.

Cover photo: Skjold Photographs

Faith Alive Christian Resources published by CRC Publications. Discover Your Bible series. *Discover Genesis: Abraham and Sarah,* © 1989, 2001, CRC Publications, 2850 Kalamazoo Ave. SE, Grand Rapids, MI 49560. All rights reserved. Printed in the United States of America on recycled paper. ✆

We welcome your comments. Call us at 1-800-333-8300 or e-mail us at editors@faithaliveresources.org.

ISBN 1-56212-145-6

10 9 8 7 6 5 4 3 2

# Contents

# To the Leader

**Prepare the Lesson**

This leader guide is meant to assist small group leaders, not to substitute for your own personal work. Always answer the study guide questions first, using the suggested basic steps of preparation. Then use the leader material to enrich your understanding of the passage.

Do not take the leader guide to the Bible study group. You do not want to give the impression that you have an answer book. The answers are in the Bible; you are a guide to help your group find the answers in God's Word.

Prepare thoroughly before each group session so that you can lead without frequent references to your notes. This will leave you free to concentrate on your leadership responsibilities. You will also be able to keep better eye contact and listen more carefully.

**Get Ready to Lead**

Learn to think in questions. As you prepare the lesson, ask yourself questions and discover your own answers. There is no better way to prepare yourself to anticipate the group's questions and help others discover truths from God's Word.

**Lead with Questions**

Use questions to direct the discussion. Draw out positive contributions with questions. Break down difficult or unclear questions with smaller, concise questions. Respond to wrong answers or problems with questions. If you learn to lead others to the truth by questions, you will be a good Bible discovery leader. The questions in this study are designed to be used with the New International Version of the Bible, but other translations can be used too.

**Help to Apply**

Gently help group members discover the meaning of God's message for their own lives. Be careful not to be judgmental of those who are not yet applying these truths. It's the Spirit's work to apply God's Word to the hearts of men and women. Tactfully let the group know how the Spirit is applying it in your heart and life. Pray faithfully for the Spirit's work in others.

Keep application low-key. Be careful not to put any personal pressure on group members to apply the truths. Simply try to help group members see that there is a relationship between the Bible and life. Avoid the use of direct pronouns in application. For example, instead of asking, "What does this mean to you?" ask, "What does this mean in our lives?" or instead of asking, "What will you do?" ask, "What action does this passage suggest?"

## Leadership Training

If there is more than one group, leaders are strongly encouraged to meet regularly for discussion of the lesson, for prayer, and for mutual support. Every leader should have a copy of the book *Coffee Break Evangelism Manual with Director's Handbook*—a basic "how-to" for establishing and leading a Bible discovery group. Reread the book or portions of it periodically and review it at the beginning of each season. *Leading with Love* in the Coffee Break Core Values series is another important tool for leadership development. Leaders will also find it helpful to attend one of the many leadership training workshops offered each year. For more information on materials or training, write to Discover Your Bible, 2850 Kalamazoo Ave. SE, Grand Rapids, MI 49560 or P.O. Box 5070, STN LCD 1, Burlington, ON L7R 3Y8 or visit www.FaithAliveResources.org.

# Introduction

*Genesis* is the Greek word for "origin" or "beginning." This first book of the Bible is about beginnings. It records the beginning of the universe, of humanity, of human sin, of salvation, of civilization. In fact, Genesis is a book of beginnings of just about everything but God. God has always existed, even before the beginning of time. The author of Genesis assumes God's existence; he does not explain it. The Lord is the only God; God alone is ruler over all that exists.

The first section of this three-part study covered the creation of the world and the gradual spread of humanity over the face of the earth. It looked at humankind's rebellion against God's laws and the resulting evil and grief that came upon the human race.

This study (Genesis 11-25) focuses on the lives of one man and one woman—Abraham and Sarah. These chapters record God's call to Abraham, asking him to leave his family and country to become the father of a new nation. In this section of Genesis we find God's promises to Abraham and Sarah and their long wait for the fulfillment of those promises. Their story is a story of faith, of trusting in the word of a faithful God even when circumstances made such faith seem foolish. It is the story of a man and his wife who struggled with doubt, fear, and uncertainty concerning God. It is the story of God's faithfulness and power in the midst of human weakness. It is the story of a faith that grew in obedience, depth, and maturity. It is the story of a birth of a nation that was called into a special relationship with God.

The author of Genesis is never specifically identified in this book; however, both Jews and Christians have long accepted Moses as the probable author. The book of Genesis—along with Exodus, Leviticus, Numbers, and Deuteronomy—is part of Jewish law, the Torah. The history recorded in this book is eventually fulfilled by Jesus of Nazareth, one of Abraham's descendants. Here is where it all begins.

# Glossary of Terms

**altar**—a stone or heap of stones on which people laid animals or produce as sacrifices to God.

**bless**—to show favor and kindness.

**burnt offering**—a sacrifice that is laid on an altar and completely burned.

**covenant**—a mutually binding agreement between two parties; usually both parties agree to accept certain responsibilities.

**curse**—to pronounce judgment on someone or something.

**faith**—taking God at his word and acting on it.

**gospel**—literally means "good news." The gospel is the good news that the sinless Son of God, Jesus Christ, has died as a sacrifice for our sins. He took the punishment for our sins upon himself, dying on the cross and rising again. After his resurrection, Jesus ascended into heaven, and he will someday return to establish his kingdom.

**judgment**—God's pronouncement that a person is either sinful or righteous.

**justified**—God's declaration that those who believe in Jesus are pardoned of sin because of Jesus' sacrifice on the cross.

**mercy**—free and undeserved compassion.

**prophecy**—a message from someone who speaks for God.

**righteous**—free from guilt or sin; perfectly conformed to God's will and moral standards.

**sacrifice**—the act of offering something precious to God. In the Old Testament this was usually an animal (the best in the flock) or the firstfruits of the harvest. Sometimes people sacrificed an animal to receive forgiveness from God; though they deserved death for their sins, God accepted the slain animal in their place. Jesus is often referred to as the "Lamb of God," the sinless Son of God who willingly died, taking on himself the punishment for the sins of the world. All who believe in him receive forgiveness from God.

**sin**—going against God's will.

**worship**—reverence and respect given to God; acknowledging God's worthiness to be praised and served.

# Lesson 1

Genesis 11:27-12:20

## The Lord Calls

### Introductory Notes

As you begin this study of Genesis, you may be faced with several problems. You are beginning in the middle of the book of Genesis. If your group has already studied Genesis 1-11, this first lesson will overlap. But if your group (or some members in your group) have not studied the first eleven chapters, you will need to spend a few minutes in this first session reviewing those chapters. Touch on the themes of creation, fall, and redemption as outlined in Genesis 1-3. As you briefly relate the story of Noah, point out that God did not abandon his creation, in spite of the disobedience and ungodliness of its inhabitants.

As you review, use questions to discover how much your group members already know. If they have a good working knowledge of Genesis 1-11, shorten your introduction accordingly. Encourage your group—whether newcomer or grow group—to read these chapters on their own.

Remember that the first eleven chapters of Genesis serve as a preface to the rest of the book. They provide the setting for the history of Abraham and Sarah and their descendants. With the introduction of Abraham, we begin a new section of the book that closely follows the events in the life of this family. Use the first four sections in this lesson to focus on how Genesis 11:27-12:9 introduces the story of Abraham.

If your group has not met together before or if you are looking for a way to help group members talk, use the Optional Opening Share Questions that are included with each lesson.

### Optional Opening Share Question

**What is your favorite season of the year? Why?**

1. *Genesis 11:27-32*

   *What do we learn about Terah's family?*

   Note how this passage is introduced (v. 27). **Why might the author have specified that this is the account of Terah, rather than that of Abram?** The emphasis on Abram's father links Abram with the historical account of Genesis 1-11 and focuses on the link between Abram and Shem (see 11:10-26). It emphasizes the importance of the family line, a line that God had singled out for his particular blessing and purpose.

This passage is divided into two sections. The first records that Terah became a parent and the head of his clan; the second tells of his journey, along with members of his family, in search of a new land. This sets the stage for Abram's own migration (12:4-5). Explore this passage with the following questions: **Who seem to be the most important people here? What do we learn about the women in Terah's family? Why might the author have included the detail about Sarai's barrenness? What move did Terah decide to make? Who went with him?**

Focus also on what this account suggests about the chapters to come. **Based on this genealogy, which people might we expect to be significant in the following chapters of Genesis?** Your group should mention Terah's care of Lot, Abram's nephew. Sarai's barrenness is also a hint of something that might play a large role in her and Abram's life.

2. *Genesis 12:1-3*

   a. *What command did the Lord give Abram?*

   b. *What did he promise in return for Abram's obedience? Who would benefit from these promises?*

Your group may wonder at the lack of explanation for the Lord's appearance to Abram. Because the text gives us no information on Abram's relationship to God prior to this, we have no way of knowing why God chose Abram, other than that he was one of Shem's descendants. However, the chapters that follow will tell us much about Abram's faith in God. The main point here is that God initiated the contact. **What does this action tell us about the Lord's relationship to Abram? What might we expect in the chapters that follow?**

Grow groups may want to compare God's call and promise here to the blessing in Genesis 1:27-30. **How do both affirm the goodness of life? Had either Adam and Eve or Abram done anything to merit these promises from God? How does God's promise to Abram counter the curse in Genesis 3:15?**

If there's time, grow groups might also explore the connections between God's call of Abram and God's call to believers today. **How is this call similar to the New Testament call to follow Jesus? (See Matt. 4:19; 19:27.) How is Abram's call unique?**

Look at the sacrifice required in God's call as well as the blessing. **What two things does God's call require Abram to leave behind? How will the blessing that follows fill that gap?** The Lord asked Abram to leave not only his country but also his father's household. However, God promised to give Abram a new country and to make him the head of a great nation. Abram would also be blessed by having special protection from others. **Why might**

**Abram have needed that protection?** Talk about the dangers of leaving behind family and friends and setting out alone to an unknown land.

Note also that God promised to make Abram a blessing to all the nations of the world. **Why is the inclusion of "all peoples on earth" important? Is anyone excluded in that phrase?** This theme is key throughout the entire Bible. It points to the day when salvation would be offered to all people— not only to Abram's descendants—through Jesus, who would also descend from Abram's line.

Verse 2 combines both command and promise. **What might God have meant by promising to make Abram's name great? What would that mean for Abram? What do you think the words** *bless* **and** *curse* **mean?** (Newcomers especially may think that cursing here means swearing or putting someone under an evil spell. Explain that the meaning intended here is closer to "calling upon divine or supernatural power to send injury upon someone.")

As you talk about God's promises, explore the reason God might have made these promises to Abram. **Does the text suggest that Abram had done anything extraordinary or outstanding? Were God's promises conditional? Did they depend on anything that Abram might or might not do?** Your group should note that God's promises were simply given to Abraham, no strings attached. Note also that the command seems rather vague: "Go to the land I will show you." **What does that tell us about the Lord's way of dealing with people at times?**

Because these verses form the basis of the story of Abram, be prepared to refer to them frequently in the next lessons.

3.   *Genesis 12:4-5*
    *a.   How did Abram respond to God's call?*
    *b.   Whom did Abram take with him?*
    *c.   To what country did they go?*

The text does not give us any idea of what Abram's previous relationship with God had been like. It does not tell us whether Abram had any hesitations in following the Lord's command or what preparations he made. However, the kind of immediate and unhesitating obedience to God implied here becomes a pattern in the life of Abram and Sarai. **How is obedience linked to one's relationship with God? What does Abram's example teach us? What can we expect of Abram in the future?**

Explore the details in these verses. **Why might Abram have taken these particular people with him? Why do you think he headed for Canaan?** Note that these questions cannot be answered from the text. But let them lead your group to imagine who Abram was and the kinds of things he faced in following God's commands.

11

4. *Genesis 12:6-9*

   a. *What promise did God make to Abram at Shechem?*
   b. *How does this promise differ from the previous ones (12:2-3)?*
   c. *What was Abram's response?*
   d. *What kind of lifestyle did Abram lead?*

Bring along a map to use as you look at these verses. Some of your group members may have maps in their Bibles. Encourage them to look for the places mentioned in this section. The cities of Shechem, Bethel, and Ai tell us that Abram was moving about in the inland hill country of Canaan rather than along the coastal plain. The Negev, though today a desert, in Abram's time had sufficient water to sustain towns and even some cultivation. Shechem was the most important Canaanite town in that area, located at the crossing of two important trade routes. The "great tree of Moreh" was probably the site of local pagan worship.

**What does the mention of towns and the note in verse 6 tell us about the land? How might this have made God's choice of Canaan seem like an unlikely gift to Abram?** Abram may have wondered how he and his descendants were going to take possession of a land already well inhabited. With one later exception, Abram never claimed any of the land of Canaan for his possession. **But how does he claim possession of the land in a symbolic way? What does this tell us about Abram's faith in God?** Note that Abram built altars as a response to God's appearing and as a place in which to offer worship ("called on the name of the Lord" is a biblical phrase used to indicate an act of public worship).

Verse 7 is the first record of God's having appeared to a person since Adam and Eve were banished from the Garden of Eden. The wording implies that God appeared physically, not simply as a voice speaking. As you talk about God's promise to Abram here, ask some of the following questions: **What makes the fulfillment of this promise unlikely? What is significant about Abram's response? What does this tell us about Abram and his belief in the Lord?**

5. *Genesis 12:10-13*

   a. *Why did Abram go to Egypt?*
   b. *What did he tell Sarai to do? Why?*

The famine was another factor that might have made Abram wonder about the land God had promised him. Much of the land of Canaan was dry; a famine could be devastating. Abram did what many in the ancient world did to escape famine; he moved to Egypt temporarily, since the land there was watered by the Nile River. (Grow groups will note that it was also a famine that brought Abram's descendants to Egypt years later, a visit that ended in more than four hundred years of slavery and oppression.) **Why might Abram not have built an altar in Egypt?** Discuss how the altars that Abram built were a response of faith to God's promise to give him and his descendants the land of Canaan; in some ways they represented God's (and Abram's) claim on the land. This would not have been appropriate in Egypt.

Your group will no doubt be intrigued by this episode in Abram and Sarai's life. **What do these verses tell us about Abram and Sarai and about the culture in which they lived? How does Abram's behavior contrast with what we've read of him earlier? How might we have expected him to behave? Why?** Abram's fear was justifiable, of course. As an alien, Abram was powerless in the Egyptian culture; he was without rights. At that time it was not the custom for women to veil themselves, so Sarah's beauty would be apparent to everyone she met. As the story indicates (v. 15), Abram's fears were justified. **How did he try to protect himself? For whom was he most fearful?** This incident gives us a glimpse into Abram's human nature, as well as insight into the culture of his day.

6. *Genesis 12:14-16*
   a. *What happened to Sarai in Egypt?*
   b. *What happened to Abram?*

Be sure that group members understand that the ruler of Egypt was referred to as the Pharaoh, a generic title. Pharaoh apparently gave Abram sheep, cattle, and other goods as payment for taking Sarai as one of his wives. In our culture, of course, this story is bound to raise questions: **How must Sarai have felt about this arrangement? Did Pharaoh actually live with her as his wife? How might Abram have felt about his decision to lie about Sarai?** We cannot answer these with certainty, of course, but it was most likely an emotional and fearful time for Abram and Sarai.

7. *Genesis 12:17-20*
   a. *What did the Lord do to Pharaoh and his household?*
   b. *What was Pharaoh's response?*

Although Abram prospered, Pharaoh did not. **Why might the Lord have acted to free Sarai? Why was she important to the fulfillment of God's promises to Abram?** The text does not say how Pharaoh knew that the disease had come on account of Sarai. Perhaps God visited him in a dream, or perhaps Sarai confessed her part in the deception. Whatever the case, Pharaoh acted quickly. He ordered Abram and Sarai to leave Egypt at once.

Note that Pharaoh did not harm Abram or take away any of his possessions. **What might have prevented Pharaoh from taking more drastic action against Abram? What did this incident tell Abram about the effectiveness of the Lord's promise in Genesis 12:3?**

Grow groups may want to compare Abram's experience in Egypt with that of the Israelites some five hundred years later. **What drew Jacob and his family to Egypt? How were they delivered from their Egyptian masters? How much wealth did they carry out of Egypt? To what land did they return?**

As you talk about Abram's experience, do so in the broader context of God's call on Abram's life. **How does this incident in Egypt contrast with Abram's obedience in following God's call? How did the Lord respond to Abram's lack of faith? What does that tell us about God? Will human faithlessness alter God's promises?** Reinforce the idea that God was faithful to his promises even when Abram made mistakes and acted in a way that showed little faith in God.

8. *Genesis 11:27-12:20*

   a. *What had the Lord promised Abram?*

   b. *How would you characterize Abram's response to the Lord?*

As you summarize this lesson, ask your group how these passages might form a preface, or introductory statement, to Abram and Sarai's story. **What was the basis of Abram's relationship to the Lord? How does this story show us different sides of Abram's belief in God's promises?**

Though Abram trusted God to fulfill his promises, circumstances seemed to indicate that those promises would not come true. **What were some of these circumstances?** Your group should recognize the fact that Canaan was already inhabited, that Abram had not as yet staked claim to any portion of the land, that Sarai remained childless, and that the trip to Egypt resulted in Sarai's being taken as the Pharaoh's wife. Circumstances certainly seemed against Abram. As you proceed through the stories that follow, your group will see that Sarai's childlessness and Abram's lack of land ownership are two key themes. Be prepared to return to this lesson in future discussions.

# Lesson 2

Genesis 13:1-14:24

# Abram and Lot

## Introductory Notes

As chapters 13 and 14 of Genesis will show us, Abram's relationship with his nephew Lot was important. After all, Abram and Sarai remained childless, and as long as Lot was a part of their family, he was the natural heir to Abram's great wealth. But perhaps God wanted Abram to rely completely on his promises for a son, or perhaps he was simply calling Abram to leave all his family behind in following God's call. Whatever God's purposes, the time had come for Abram and Lot to part ways. However, Abram did not abandon his nephew. When Lot was in trouble, Abram came to his rescue, risking his life in battle against an alliance of Canaanite kings.

The content and style of chapter 14 differs from the rest of Genesis. For example, its initial focus is on outside historical events of the period. Abram is mentioned only in the context of the role he played in the battles between the city-states of his day. The literary style of this chapter differs from the rest of Abram's history, and Abram himself is referred to as "Abram the Hebrew" (v. 13)—a somewhat insulting term used primarily by non-Israelites to distinguish the Jewish people from the Egyptians or Philistines. (This is the first time the word "Hebrew" appears in the Bible.) For these reasons, some scholars believe that this chapter was written by historians and copied into the Genesis account because of the important role Abram plays.

Despite the uniqueness of the chapter, it does teach important principles about obeying God and resisting a culture that does not worship God. Here Abram passes yet another test of his faith in God's promises.

Since this lesson is longer than usual, watch your time and avoid belaboring details that may detract from the main point of the lesson.

## Optional Opening Share Question

**Do you find it hard to be unselfish?**

1. *Genesis 13:1-4*

   *What do these verses tell us about Abram?*

Take some time to explore the details of this passage with your group. Again Abram preferred to live in the hill country and the drier land of the

Negev rather than in the greener, more inhabited areas. He did not settle in any city but rather moved from place to place. **What did he do when he returned to Bethel? Why might that be important? What does that tell us about Abram's relationship to God, especially after his stay in Egypt?** Talk about Abram's faithfulness in his worship of God. **How does his "calling on the name of the Lord" reflect his faith in God's promises?**

2. *Genesis 13:5-7*

   *What began to affect the relationship between Abram and Lot?*

   At this point the previous references to Lot will take on more meaning. **What do we already know about Lot? What was his relationship to Abram? How might Sarai's childlessness have made this an especially significant relationship?** Your group should understand that Lot, Abram's nephew, was a logical heir to Abram as long as Sarai remained childless.

   Note also the comment in verse 7b. **How does this help to explain the conflict between Abram and Lot?** This verse reminds us that the two men were dividing land that was already inhabited and not theirs to divide.

3. *Genesis 13:8-9*

   *What did Abram suggest as a solution to their problem?*

   The two men stand on a bluff, overlooking the land of the Jordan River valley. Abram proposes to Lot that they separate and pasture their flocks in different areas. At that time the plain around the Jordan was very fertile (v. 10) in contrast to the dry hills on which they had been pasturing their flocks. It must have looked attractive to both men, but Abram gave his nephew the first choice of the land, even though the older man had the right to choose first. **What does this tell us about Abram?**

   In this separation Abram cuts the last of his family ties, the final act of leaving his father's household. **What does this tell us of Abram's faith that God would still provide him an heir?** Look also at the decision that Lot faced. **What does Lot's willingness to move away from God's promises to Abram tell us about him?**

4. *Genesis 13:10-13*

   a. *Why did Lot choose the plain of the Jordan?*
   b. *What does his choice tell us about him?*

   The Jordan River valley was lush and green. The biblical account compares it to the Garden of Eden and the fertile land along the Nile River in Egypt. Lot knew that whoever chose the Jordan plain would have a much easier time watering and pasturing large herds and flocks. **How does his** decision contrast with Abram's generosity in offering him the first choice? Where was Lot's first priority?

Look also at the people who had settled on the plain. So far in this study the author of Genesis has not focused on humankind's wickedness. The description of Sodom, however, reminds us of the sin and wickedness that often dominated Genesis 1-11, especially the account of the flood. **How had the Lord dealt with human wickedness in the past? What might we expect to happen to Sodom? How does verse 10 hint at the connection between Sodom's sin and the Lord's punishment?**

5. *Genesis 13:14-18*

   a. *What did the Lord promise to Abram?*

   b. *How do these promises differ from those in 12:2-3? How are they the same?*

   c. *What did the Lord ask Abram to do?*

   d. *How did Abram respond?*

God repeats his promises of blessing to Abram. **What patterns are emerging in these promises? What is repeated? What is added? Why might God have timed his appearing to Abram as he did?** Each time Abram faced separation, alienation, or hardship, the Lord assured him of blessing, land, and many descendants.

Compare verses 13 and 18. **What contrast do we find between the places Lot and Abram chose to dwell? What might this suggest about the futures of Abram and Lot?**

6. *Genesis 13:1-18*

   a. *What differences have you noticed between Abram and Lot?*

   b. *What might account for these differences?*

   c. *How did God show his continued faithfulness to Abram?*

Use these questions to summarize the division between Lot and Abram and the deeper issues that lay behind this separation. Emphasize again the theme of God's choosing one family line to bless and the growing evidence of Abram's trust in God's promises. Focus also on the differences in faith and in character between Lot and Abram as suggested in this chapter. Help your group to see that God chooses to work through those who are faithful to his commands and who trust his promises. **How would you describe the interaction between God and Abram?**

7. *Genesis 14:1-12*

   a. *What was the political situation in which Abram and Lot lived?*

   b. *How did Kedorlaomer respond to the rebellion?*

   c. *What happened to the kings of Sodom and Gomorrah?*

   d. *What detail explains why this incident is included in Abram's history?*

Don't spend too much time on this section, which gives detailed background to the main narrative: Abram's rescue of Lot and his meeting with Melchizedek and the king of Sodom.

The kings mentioned in this passage are not clearly identified with any known historical figures, but the sort of political alliance of city-states described here was typical of this period of history. The first king mentioned, Amraphel, may have been a successor to the Nimrod mentioned in Genesis 10:8-12, who had earlier forged out a kingdom in Shinar. The rebellion of the five city-states is also typical of the conquest and counter-rebellion of this period. **What does the number of kings in this passage suggest about the size of their "kingdoms"?** These were very likely small city-states (small areas of the country dominated by a large city and ruled by a tribal chieftain). **What does the unrest and instability of these times tell us of the importance of God's promise to protect Abram (12:3)?**

Kedorlaomer and his allies invaded the rebellious territories after conquering a number of other territories (vv. 5-7). The Valley of Siddim was chosen as a battleground (which may seem a poor choice, since it was full of tar pits—pools of tar that trapped living creatures in their sticky depths). Kedorlaomer soundly defeated the kings of Sodom and Gomorrah. As we read verse 12, we begin to realize the reason for this historical account: Lot was captured. **Why was Lot among the captives? Where had he chosen to live? What does this indicate about the kind of choice Lot had made?** Apparently Lot had taken up residence in the city of Sodom. **What does this tell us about him, knowing what we do about that city? How does this contrast with Abram's choices?**

8. *Genesis 14:13-16*

   a. *How did Abram become involved in the political scene?*

   b. *What did he do?*

   c. *What did he achieve as a result?*

This is the only time in Genesis that Abram is portrayed as a military figure with allies and trained fighting men. Abram responded swiftly to the news of Lot's capture. Though his fighting force seems small by our standards, it may have been large for the population at his time. However, Abram was attacking a powerful alliance of four kings who had just defeated an army of five kings. **What does Abram's victory tell us about his** courage? **About God's promise to bless and protect him?** Abram recovered all the goods and captives, attacking the armies at night at the outer edge of the promised land.

9. *Genesis 14:17-24*

   a. *What two kings came to meet Abram? How were they different?*
   b. *Whom did Melchizedek bless?*
   c. *How did Abram respond to the king of Sodom?*
   d. *Why do you think he responded this way?*

This passage is difficult to understand. Depending on the backgrounds of your group members, your discussion may yield various interpretations. For the sake of clarity, focus on the difference between the two kings. **How is Melchizedek described? Whom did he serve and worship? What did he acknowledge about Abram and about the battle that Abram had just fought?** Not only did Melchizedek believe in the one true God but he also served as a priest of God (it was not uncommon for kings of that time to function as priests). His simple act of hospitality—offering the weary Abram bread and wine—reveals graciousness and respect. (The name Melchizedek means "king of righteousness" and Salem means "peace.") It is something of a mystery that Melchizedek would recognize and serve the one true God in a pagan Canaanite culture with an understanding of God that was far less complete than Abram's. It is also curious that Abram would give Melchizedek a tenth of all that he had gotten from his attack on the kings. This tithe seems to indicate that Melchizedek was greater than Abram, as does the fact that Melchizedek blessed Abram.

Grow groups should note that Melchizedek is mentioned elsewhere in the Bible: Psalm 110:4; Hebrews 5:6-11; and Hebrews 7. Because he was both king and priest, Melchizedek is considered a forerunner or type of Christ, who is forever King and Priest for his people. If you have time, read these passages with your group, since they link this seemingly isolated historical event in Abram's life with Jesus Christ. (This connection may be too obscure for newcomer groups.) In any case, don't spend too much time on this point, since it is not central to the primary focus of the lesson.

The king of Sodom stands in contrast to Melchizedek, king of Salem. **What do we know already of Sodom? What might the ruler of such a city be like?** Refer your group to Genesis 13:13: "Now the men of Sodom were wicked and were sinning greatly against the LORD." You might also mention that chapters 18 and 19 describe more fully the wickedness of this city. **What might this have had to do with Abram's response to the king's proposal?**

**What did the king of Sodom propose to Abram? What reasons did Abram give for refusing?** The king of Sodom recognized that Abram, as the victor who had defeated Kedorlaomer, had a right to keep the booty. He did request that Abram return the people of Sodom to their homes, but the possessions that had been rescued from the battle belonged to Abram. But Abram emphatically refused them: "I will accept nothing belonging to you, not even a thread or the thong of a sandal" (14:23). As the *NIV Study Bible* notes, "Abram refused to let himself become obligated to anyone but the Lord. Had he done so, this Canaanite king might later have claimed the right of kingship over Abram."

10. *Genesis 13:1–14:24*

   a. *What does this chapter tell us about the connection between personal choices and the Lord's blessing?*

   b. *How did Abram and Lot each illustrate a different relationship to the Lord?*

**What did Abram's oath tell the king of Sodom about Abram and about Abram's God? What do the two incidents in this chapter tell us about Abram's faith?** Use these questions to tie the events of this chapter together.

Also discuss the themes of chapters 13 and 14 together: **How did Lot's choice of land and residence contrast with Abram's? How did Lot buy into the worldly quest for material wealth and greed? How does this contrast with Abram's oath to God? What do we learn in this lesson about Abram? About Lot? About God? On what is each man's relationship to God based?** Remind your group that the story of Lot is not finished; later lessons will touch on these themes again.

# Lesson 3
Genesis 15:1-21

# The Lord's Covenant

## Introductory Notes

The language of this chapter is official; it is a legal pronouncement of the inheritance God was giving to Abram. Three sections make up this chapter: God's declarations of promise, Abram's doubts, and God's reassurance. Note that the Lord repeats key words in Abram's questions as he seeks to reassure Abram of the surety of his promises: *heir* (see 15:3) in verse 4 and *know* (see 15:8) in verse 13.

## Optional Opening Share Question

**Do you find it hard to believe what you cannot see?**

1. *Genesis 15:1-3, 7*
   a. *In what new ways did the Lord identify himself to Abram here?*
   b. *What is the reason for Abram's response?*

The Lord's appearing to Abram seems to continue his message of assurance to Abram after Lot's departure (see lesson 2). So you might begin this study by noting the verses that immediately precede chapter 15. **What had Abram said to the king of Sodom? In what way did this statement demonstrate Abram's faith? Why might the Lord have appeared to Abram "after this" (15:1)? What does "after this" refer to?** As God had done earlier in times of doubt and upheaval in Abram's life, he appeared to Abram to reaffirm his promises and to strengthen Abram's faith.

Note Abram's sense of frustration (vv. 2-3) as he questioned whether God would actually fulfill his promises. **What were some hindrances to God's fulfilling his promises to Abram? What does this tell us about faith? Is it always easy? Do people of faith ever get discouraged or impatient? Why?**

You may need to explain two expressions: *word of the Lord* and *shield* and *great reward*. Both are common in the Old Testament. *Word of the Lord* is used to introduce statements that come from the prophets (people who are given messages from the Lord to proclaim to others). Grow groups may be interested to know that this is the only time this phrase occurs in Genesis; its use suggests that Abram was considered a prophet of the Lord. (You will have more opportunity to discuss this in Gen. 20.)

*Shield* and *great reward* are word pictures. **What do they tell us about the Lord? What do they say about the Lord's relationship to Abram? How do these images apply to Abram's experiences recorded in Genesis 14?** You may find it helpful to read Psalm 3:1-3 and 19:7-11 with your group. *Shield* suggests the protection of a king and was perhaps meant to reassure Abram that God would provide better protection than the king of Sodom or Melchizedek, the king of Salem. *Reward* suggests that God had heard Abram's statement to the king of Sodom (14:22-23) and would reward him for his statement of faith in God.

2. **Genesis 15:4-6**

   a. *How did God expand on his earlier promises to Abram? (See Gen. 12:1-3 and 13:14-17.)*

   b. *What was Abram's response?*

   c. *How did the Lord credit Abram's belief?*

God did not make any basic changes in his promise that Abram would have an heir. He did, however, get more specific: Abram would have a son—a natural son, not an adopted one. God also expanded on his promise of many descendants: Abram's family would be as numerous as the stars thickly clustered in the night sky. This visual illustration dramatically emphasized God's assurance of Abram's future.

Verse 6 is a key verse in Abram's story. For the first time, the word *belief* is linked to righteousness. If your group has just finished studying Genesis 1-11, you might refer them to the example of righteous Noah (Gen. 6). **How did Noah's life display this quality?** Check the glossary and discuss the definition of *righteous* given there. Then look again at Abram's belief, which God "credited as righteousness." **Did God pronounce Abram righteous because of any great deeds he had done? Because of his building altars or his formal acts of worship?** Help your group to see that God responded to Abram's attitude of heartfelt trust (the root meaning of the word *belief*). It was this belief that made Abram righteous in God's eyes.

This link between belief and righteousness is one of the most important themes in the Old and New Testaments. Grow groups may want to explore some of the New Testament passages that relate specifically to this passage in Genesis: Romans 4:1-8; Galatians 3:6-9; James 2:20-24. You may also want to touch on these passages in your newcomer groups if you feel confident that members will not be confused by the theological language used here: *faith, righteous, justified, gospel, works,* and so on. Be sure that you don't assume too much knowledge from your newcomers. Explain verse 6 as simply as you can: God declared Abram righteous (free from guilt or sin) because of Abram's heartfelt trust in God (not because of any great deeds Abram had done). You may want to mention that God offers the same declaration of righteousness to anyone who puts heartfelt trust in God through faith in Jesus. Be sensitive to the leading of God's Spirit here, since some newcomers may not yet be ready or able to hear this.

3.   *Genesis 15:7-11*

    a.   *What did Abram ask God for?*

    b.   *What did God ask him to do?*

The conversation between Abram and God (especially vv. 7-8) is very formal. This kind of language was used to draw up treaties between kings in Abram's day. In such treaties, one party would often ask the other for a sign that would confirm his part of the bargain. Here Abram asks God for such a sign. **Why might Abram have felt the need for such a sign?**

The Lord responded by making a covenant with Abram, which in those days often involved a special ceremony. An animal (or several animals) would be killed and cut in two, and the halves of their bodies would be laid opposite each other with a pathway between. The persons making the covenant would then walk between the carcasses, thus signifying their intention to keep their word: "May it be so done to me if I do not keep my oath and pledge." The Lord requested Abram to prepare the animals for this kind of covenant-making ceremony. (For another Old Testament reference to this kind of ceremony, see Jer. 34:18-20.)

4.   *Genesis 15:12-16*

    a.   *What happened to Abram?*

    b.   *What did the Lord tell Abram about the future of his descendants?*

Usually both parties involved actively participated in making a covenant, each promising certain things and passing through the halves of the slain animals. Here, however, this was not the case. Abram fell into a "deep sleep" (the same term used to describe Adam's sleep during the creation of Eve). **How actively did Abram participate in the making of this covenant? Who initiated these proceedings?** Note that even as Adam received Eve, Abram received this covenant as a result of the Lord's work, not something of his own doing.

The phrase "go to your fathers" (v. 15) means to join one's ancestors in death after a long, full life; it was seen as a blessing from God. But Abram would not live to see his family inherit the land of Canaan. **What reason did the Lord give for postponing the inheritance of Canaan to Abram's descendants until the fourth generation?** The Lord suggested that he was holding back from granting Abram the land of Canaan because the wickedness of the Amorites (who inhabited Canaan) had not reached its greatest height. **What did the wickedness of the inhabitants have to do with Abram's descendants inheriting the land?** Perhaps God wanted not only to reward Abram's family for their faithfulness to him but also to punish the peoples who had turned away from him to do evil.

If your group has difficulty understanding the concept of the Lord's judgment, take some time to explore it. **How do God's words here give a sense of his mercy as well as his judgment? Why might he have waited to destroy the Amorites? What does this tell us about the Lord? About his concern even for people who do wickedness?** For a New Testament perspective on God's judgment and mercy, see 1 Thessalonians 2:14-16 and 2 Peter 3:3-9.

God revealed to Abram that his descendants would be captives before they became conquerors. This is the only time that the events recorded in Exodus are mentioned in the book of Genesis. Discuss God's prophecy concerning the future. **What do these words tell us about God? About God's knowledge of and control over the future?** Prophecy and fulfillment are two major biblical themes; God used them repeatedly to teach people that God knows and controls the future and holds all things in his powerful hands. Hopefully your group members will begin to see this as they study this passage. (Grow groups may want to compare God's prophecy with the events they remember of the Israelites' stay in Egypt.)

5. *Genesis 15:17-21*

    a. *What happened at sundown?*

    b. *What covenant did God make with Abram?*

God finalized or sealed his covenant agreement with Abram by passing between the halves of the slaughtered animals. As usual, God did not appear in full majesty and splendor but rather clothed himself with a form that symbolized his presence. God appeared as fire and smoke, both of which are used often throughout the Bible to symbolize God's presence. **What tells us that this covenant is of the Lord's making, not of Abram's? Did Abram also make a promise and walk between the halves of the slain animals? Did God require anything of Abram in return for the covenant promise?** As you discuss these questions, talk about the meaning of the word *covenant* (see the glossary). Note that covenants usually involved two parties who made promises to each other. **Is that true of this covenant as well? What might this tell us about God and about his relationship to Abram?** Note that God freely offered Abram his blessing and love with no demand that Abram give anything in return. (Grow groups may want to compare this with the covenant of grace and forgiveness God offers through Jesus Christ. **How are the two similar? How does each link faith and righteousness? What does this tell us about the believer's relationship with God?**)

If your group has studied Genesis 1-11, be sure to mention God's covenant with Noah (Gen. 9:8-17). If there's time, invite your group to explore the similarities between the two: **How does the Bible describe both Abram and Noah? What characterized their relationship with God? How do these covenants express God's continuing faithfulness and care? Does either of these covenants require anything in return?**

Some in your group may wonder if Abram was disappointed when God said that the promises would be postponed. Discuss this, using the following questions: **Had God answered Abram's desire to "know" (v. 8)? How did God explain the postponement to Abram? What more specific information did he give Abram concerning the promised inheritance?** God gave some very specific boundaries to the promised land, identifying the rivers that would bound the territory and naming the tribes that inhabited that area. Again, your group may be interested to know that God's Word was completely fulfilled, since the description includes all of the land that Israel's greatest kings, David and Solomon, held at the height of their kingdoms (see 1 Kings 4:21).

6.  *Genesis 15:1-21*

    *What was the basis for the relationship between Abram and the Lord?*

As you review this important lesson, take time to explore the relationship between belief and righteousness. **How does this story illustrate that relationship? What confidence could Abram put in this covenant with God? How had this confidence shaped his life up to this point?**

Don't leave this discussion only at the level of God's relationship with Abram. Ask other questions to help your group begin to apply these truths to their own relationship with God: **How is belief in God's promises basic to a person's relationship to God? How is one able to believe? What are some promises God offers to people today?** If you are leading a newcomer group, be careful not to rush through these more personal questions. Be alert to any group members who may be struggling with these concepts or who may want to speak with you privately at the end of your session.

# Lesson 4

Genesis 16:1-16

## The Servant's Son

### Introductory Notes

The story of the birth of Abram's first son immediately follows God's renewal of his promise to provide Abram with an heir (15:4). As you discuss this lesson, note how Abram and Sarai sought to solve their childlessness. **In what earlier incident have we seen Abram and Sarai trying on their own to solve a predicament?** Your group members will probably remember this couple's deception in Egypt when they foolishly tried their own ingenuity rather than trusting God's care and promises.

### Optional Opening Share Question

**When you were a child did you ever run away from home?**

1. *Genesis 16:1-6*

   a. *What problem still stood in the way of the Lord's promise of an heir?*

   b. *Why do you think Sarai tried to solve that problem?*

   c. *What happened as a result?*

This chapter may seem strange to group members who live in a culture far different from that of Abram and Sarai. To help your group understand why Abram and Sarai acted as they did, you may want to include some of the following information in your discussion. However, get group members' reactions from the passage first and offer background information only as needed.

**How might Sarai have been feeling about her continuing infertility? How did her society view women who were unable to bear children?** Sarai must have experienced much grief and frustration about her childlessness. It was extremely important in that time to have an heir to inherit the family wealth, to carry on the family name, and to care for aging parents. In addition, childlessness at that time was thought to be the woman's fault; barren women were often taunted and mistreated. No doubt Sarai's desire for a child and her grief at remaining childless were equal to Abram's. According to her society, she had brought shame to her husband's family and name.

The culture of Sarai's day, however, allowed women a way out of such a predicament. If a barren wife owned a female slave as her personal maid, the wife could offer that slave to her husband as a kind of surrogate wife. If the slave conceived and bore a child, that child was considered the property of the wife and could be claimed as a legal heir. The ancient laws stipulated that the slave woman became the property of the husband and was given a higher status than that of a mere slave. **How does Sarai's idea seem to be a good solution to her predicament? Did Sarai and Abram have any reason to think that this was not a legitimate way to solve the problem? Had God specified that Sarai would be the mother of the promised child?** Though your group may tend to criticize Abram and Sarai's actions, they should understand the role that culture plays.

Look carefully at Sarai's words in verse 2: "The Lord has kept me ... ," "perhaps I can build a family. . . ." **What was Sarai implying about God? Where had she put her trust, after waiting so long in vain for God to fulfill his promise?**

Sarai's plan worked, but it did not achieve what she had hoped. **What happened when Hagar became pregnant? How did she begin to treat Sarai? What did Sarai do in response?** Hagar began to flaunt her pregnancy in front of Sarai. Jealous and hurt, Sarai appealed to Abram as the head of the house to restore peace. And Abram responded by giving Hagar back into Sarai's hands. (The legal code of that day punished such female servants by reducing them to slave status again.) Sarai must have been quite harsh with Hagar. Abram's household had become a place of tension, resentment, and jealousy as a result of Sarai's plan. **What does this suggest about trying to work God's will out in our own way and our own timing?**

2. *Genesis 16:7-10*

   a. *What did the angel call Hagar? How is Sarai identified in these verses?*

   b. *Describe the angel's confrontation with Hagar. What command and promise did he give her?*

Hagar likely was returning to her native country (Shur was a town near the border of Canaan and Egypt) and taking her son away from the promised land. **What does this suggest about her son's status as the "promised son"?**

The passage tells us that an "angel of the Lord" found Hagar, the first time Genesis records a meeting between an angel and a human being. It is significant that the first person we read of being visited by an angel is an Egyptian servant woman, a runaway slave. **What might that tell us about God? About God's concern for all people?**

The angel spoke compassionately to Hagar. God sought out this runaway slave, as God had earlier sought out disobedient Adam and Eve and Cain, the murderer. **How did the angel address Hagar? What does that suggest about her situation? How did Hagar herself acknowledge this? How did she identify Sarai (v. 8)?** The conversation emphasizes that Sarai's claim on Hagar and her child was legitimate.

However, the angel made a promise to Hagar and her unborn child implying that Hagar would have her own family. Her son would not be the child of promise. The boy would be blessed, but not because of his relationship to Sarai. This suggests that the son of promise would be Sarai's true son, not an adopted one.

3. *Genesis 16:11-14*

 a. *How did the angel describe Hagar's child?*
 b. *What did Hagar name the well? Why was this significant?*

The angel's description of Ishmael is vivid: "a wild donkey of a man." **What other words describe Ishmael's character? What do we learn about his future and the future of his descendants?** According to the angel, there would be hostility between Ishmael and Abram's promised heir. In fact, Ishmael would live in peace with no one. And, like the wild donkeys that roamed the desert, Ishmael would wander all his life. Though the descendants of Abram's promised son would eventually settle in the land of Canaan, Ishmael's sons would not have a land to call their own. (Most commentaries agree that the Bedouins are descended from Ishmael; they are proud and spirited, a wandering people who serve no one.)

Two names are significant in this passage. The first is Ishmael, which, as the angel suggests (v. 11), means "the Lord hears." **Why was this an appropriate name? What would it remind Hagar of in the years to come?** The second is the name of the well, which Hagar called *Beer Lahai Roi*. Although the meaning of the Hebrew is uncertain, most scholars agree that it means something like "the God who sees" or "the One who sees me." **What does this tell us about Hagar's relationship to the Lord? About her trust in him? What had she learned about God's character?**

4. *Genesis 16:15-16*

 *How does the story end?*

These verses clearly establish Ishmael as Abram and Hagar's—not Sarai's—son. We also find that Ishmael received the name that the angel had spoken to Hagar.

Note that the author carefully establishes Abram's age at the time of Ishmael's birth. **Why is this detail important? How does it explain Sarai's fear that time was running out? How long had Abram and Sarai been in Canaan?** The next lesson will focus on Abram's age in regard to faith in

God's promises. **What good had Sarai's plan done? Did the problems between Hagar and Sarai remain?**

5. *Genesis 16:1-16*
   a. *What does this chapter teach us about the Lord's character?*
   b. *What does it teach us about taking God's will into our own hands?*

As we saw in the case of Hagar, the Lord seeks those who are lost. **What other examples of this teaching do we find in Genesis 1-11? What might this mean for us today?** Your group may find it helpful to explore this theme in the New Testament as well, particularly in the three parables of Luke 15: the lost sheep, the lost coin, and the lost son.

Also tie in the theme mentioned at the beginning of this lesson: that things often go wrong when we take God's promises into our own hands and try to bring them about without waiting for God. **How was this true in the incidents we studied in this lesson? What might be some examples from our own lives?**

# Lesson 5

Genesis 17:1-27

## The Sign of the Covenant

### Introductory Notes

This chapter builds on two themes found in Genesis 15: Abram's faith and God's grace. God had made a covenant with Abram, confirming it by a special ceremony. You might review chapter 15 briefly with your group to make sure they remember the terms of that covenant.

There are some differences between chapters 15 and 17, however. In chapter 17 your group will discover that God asked something of Abram— or Abraham, as we must now call him. The covenant, a mutual exchange of promises, would bind Abraham to obedience to God. Note also that God emphasized the promise of his presence with Abraham and his descendants, rather than the promise of land.

### Optional Opening Share Question

**Does your family do anything symbolic?**

1. *Genesis 17:1-2*
   a. *How many years had passed since the birth of Ishmael? (See 16:16.)*
   b. *How did the Lord identify himself to Abram?*
   c. *What did the Lord ask of Abram? What do you think that means?*

Though the events in chapters 16 and 17 seem to follow in quick succession, make sure your group notes that thirteen years had passed since Ishmael's birth. Abram had been in Canaan well over twenty years, and still there was no sign of God's fulfilling the promise of a child. **How might Abram have been feeling at this point?** As verses 17-18 suggest, Abram had probably given up expecting a natural heir and hoped that Ishmael could be that promised son.

Look also at the way God identified himself to Abram: "God Almighty." This is the first time in Genesis that God has named himself. This name (which in Hebrew is *El Shaddai*) emphasizes God's power and ability to live up to his promises. This name for God is often used in situations where people are helpless and need reassurance. Talk about the meaning of *almighty*: "having absolute power over all" (Webster's). **Given the events of Genesis 16, why might the Lord have used this name here? What was he** telling Abram? Why might the Lord have declared his name before he gave a promise or command?

God said, "I will confirm my covenant between me and you" (v. 2). Briefly review what that covenant was. **What is the meaning of the word** *covenant*? **What were the terms of the agreement between God and Abram (see Gen. 15)?** As you discuss this, ask your group to count how many times the phrase *my covenant* appears in chapter 17. **What might this tell us about the covenant God had established with Abram? Who initiated that covenant? Who was making the promises?**

Note also that God asked Abram to "walk before me and be blameless" (v. 1). If your group has already studied Genesis 1-11, ask where else in the book of Genesis members have seen the word *walk* used in this way. Refer to the examples of Enoch and Noah (Gen. 5:24; 6:9). **What does it mean to "walk before God"? How can one be blameless in God's eyes? How might this blamelessness be related to the righteousness Abram gained through his faith in God (Gen. 15:6)?** God was asking of Abram not just good moral conduct but an entire life devoted to the Lord, a life of trust and obedience.

2. *Genesis 17:3-8*

   a. *What things did God promise Abram?*
   b. *Why did he change Abram's name?*

Verses 3-21 are a detailed account of God's conversation with Abram. They present new content in God's covenant with Abram and contain instructions as to how Abram was to carry out the covenant. God promised Abram an heir, land to inherit, and an eternal relationship with God. Look especially at verse 7, which is considered the heart of God's covenant with Abram. **What did God promise? How long would the covenant be effective? How would you describe the relationship God promised to have with Abram and all his descendants? Why might this be considered the heart of the covenant, something more basic than the promise of land or an heir?** Talk about what it means for God to say to someone, "I will be your God." This implies God's protection, blessing, and friendship given to that person—and his or her faithful worship of and love for God.

If your group is using the New International Version in this study, have members look at the footnotes explaining the meaning of the names Abram ("exalted father") and Abraham ("father of many"). **Why is this change significant? What does it have to do with the covenant between God and Abraham?** (Grow groups may note that God sometimes changed a person's name to signify an important milestone in his or her relationship to God: Abram to Abraham, Sarai to Sarah, Jacob to Israel, Simon to Peter, and so on.)

Your group may want to speculate how this covenant with Abraham applies to present-day Israel. Encourage them instead to apply this covenant to Abraham's spiritual descendants, those who live by faith in God. Use passages such as Romans 4:16-25; Galatians 3:29; and Revelation 7:9 to help them see that Abraham's spiritual family embraces people from every tribe and language. Abraham became, as God had promised, "a father of many nations" (v. 5).

3. *Genesis 17:9-14*
   a. *How was Abraham to keep God's covenant?*
   b. *Who was involved in keeping God's covenant?*
   c. *How long would that covenant last?*

If you have group members who are unfamiliar with circumcision, explain that circumcision involves cutting away the foreskin of the penis. The procedure sometimes is done for religious reasons but more often for the sake of cleanliness. **Why might circumcision have been an appropriate sign of the covenant?** Most people groups of Abraham's day circumcised adult men; the Israelites were unique in their circumcision of infants.

**What did circumcision mean for Abraham and his family? What significance had God placed on this rite?** God had called Abraham to a blameless and faithful life of fellowship with him. Circumcision was a sign that Abraham accepted this life of obedience. Note also that God insisted on even infants being circumcised. **What does this imply about God's covenant? About those who are included in it? What does this mean for a child who is circumcised long before he has made any conscious decision to live in faithfulness to God's covenant?** Circumcised infants had no choice in the matter. In this way the Lord reminded his people that he was the one who initiated and upheld the covenant relationship with them. He had chosen them before they were able to choose him.

Some group members may wonder why the sign of the covenant was limited only to males. Didn't women belong too? The answer is that women were indeed included in the covenant, but in the culture of that day (and throughout much of history) males represented the household. Women were always seen as extensions of male authority.

**Was the sign of circumcision only for those born of Abraham's flesh and blood?** Read verses 12-13. **Whom does this command include?** All of Abraham's male servants and slaves, regardless of their nationality or race, were to receive the sign of circumcision. **How might this be related to God's promise that Abraham would be a blessing to all nations?** This theme is echoed throughout the Old Testament in such passages as Isaiah 2:1-4. It is fulfilled in God's offer of salvation to all people through faith in Jesus (see Matt. 28:18-20; Eph. 1:11-13).

Note also that circumcision meant a commitment to God's people. **If one of Abraham's descendents were not circumcised, what would happen to him (v. 14)? What might be the reason for such an emphasis on community?** Help your group to see that God does not work solely with individuals; here God emphasizes his covenant with an entire family line and household stretching over many generations.

Your group may have questions about the need for the sign of circumcision today. Explain that God's covenant with Abraham was established during the time of the Old Testament—before Christ's coming. During this time God used physical signs (like circumcision, sacrifices, and so on) to symbolize an inner spiritual reality (faith in God, commitment to his covenant, forgiveness of sins, and so on). Circumcision symbolized a willingness to "walk blameless before God." When Jesus came, however, he taught that the inner spiritual reality was more important than exterior ritual. The rites and practices of the Old Testament law are no longer required of the Christian. As Paul says, "For in Christ Jesus neither circumcision nor uncircumcision has any value. The only thing that counts is faith expressing itself in love" (Gal. 5:6).

4. *Genesis 17:15-16*

   a.  *What did God promise to Sarai?*

   b.  *Why did he change her name?*

Sarai was also included in God's covenant promises to Abraham. **What might have been God's reason for naming her specifically here? What does this tell us about Ishmael? What relationship would Sarai's son have to Ishmael?** Sarah was now assured that her own son would have a special place over Ishmael.

The names Sarai and Sarah both mean "princess." Evidently God renamed Sarai to emphasize that she would be the mother of kings (see v. 16). As noted earlier in this study, a name change often marked a significant change in one's relationship with God. It was God's way of affirming his continuing presence and purpose in a person's life. Given the place of women in that society, it's interesting that God affirmed Sarah even as he had affirmed Abraham.

5. *Genesis 17:17-18*

   *What does Abraham's response indicate about his belief in God?*

**What does Abraham's falling face down tell us about his attitude toward God?** Lying prostrate was a gesture of deep reverence and worship. Abraham held God in respect and awe. He acknowledged that God was worthy of his worship.

Abraham's reaction to God's words, however, was one of belief mixed with doubt. **What might have been the reasons for his doubt? For his faith? How does this passage relate to Genesis 15:6?** Abraham's laughter was not necessarily mocking; it may have been simply that the thought of two such old people having a baby made Abraham chuckle. His respectful request to God was spoken with a tone of longing: "If only Ishmael might live under your blessing!" Abraham obviously desired an end to this long wait for an heir, and he loved Ishmael. **What effect, however, might this long wait have had on Abraham's faith? How might it have changed the focus of his thinking?**

Remind your group of Abraham's laughter when you discuss the birth of Isaac, whose name means "he laughs."

6. *Genesis 17:19-22*

   a. *What did God promise for Ishmael? Why?*

   b. *In what ways would Isaac be special?*

God's answer regarding Ishmael ("I have heard you: I will surely bless him") was a play on Ishmael's name, which means "the Lord hears." The Lord's promise (v. 20) was fulfilled, as we read in Genesis 25:12-16.

But Isaac would be the son of promise. The son whose name means "he laughs" would bring the kind of joy that the Lord had promised to Abraham. **How did God emphasize that Isaac would be the son of promise?** God's promise of a son born to Sarah, his extending the covenant to Isaac, his explanation regarding Ishmael's future, and his reaffirming the covenant with Isaac—all these confirm to Abraham that Isaac would be the son of promise. **What do we learn from this passage about the God who hears and answers prayer?**

7. *Genesis 17:23-27*

   *What do these verses tell us about Abraham?*

**How did Abraham respond to God's command (vv. 11-12)? How had Abraham's faith developed through the events of this chapter? What had he learned about God?** Abraham responded promptly to God's command with complete obedience. It may be significant that the rite of circumcision was instituted a year before Isaac's birth. Ishmael was circumcised along with the others in Abraham's household; but Isaac, the true heir of the promise, would be circumcised as a newborn.

Evidently all the males, faced with the possibility of being cut off from Abraham's household if they refused, agreed to be circumcised (v. 27).

8. *Genesis 17:1-27*

   *In what ways had the Lord demonstrated his faithfulness in keeping his covenant with Abraham?*

Use this question to weave together the themes from Genesis 15 and 17 as you review God's covenant with Abraham and Sarah. **What promises had God made? What did God require of Abraham and Sarah? What would happen to those who chose not to keep the covenant and receive the sign of circumcision? What was the basis of the covenant?** In your discussion, emphasize that God kept his part of the covenant in a way that clearly demonstrated his absolute power and complete faithfulness in spite of roadblocks and delays.

# Lesson 6

Genesis 18:1-33

## The Faithful Lord

### Introductory Notes

Because this lesson contains two stories, it might be rather lengthy. The first story repeats God's promise that Sarah will bear Abraham a son of promise. We see God as one who opens the womb of the barren woman (a theme echoed in the stories of Rachel, Hannah, Samson's mother, the Shunammite woman, and Elizabeth). The second story tells of Abraham the mediator, a man of compassion who cries out to God on behalf of his nephew Lot. Be prepared to look at God as a judge who punishes evil but who also tempers his judgment with mercy.

### Optional Opening Share Question

**How do you show hospitality to a guest?**

1. *Genesis 18:1-5*

   *What do we learn of Abraham's character in these verses?*

   In our society today, Abraham's hospitality would seem completely foolhardy. But his welcome of the three visitors was typical Mideastern hospitality of his day.

   Abraham's visitors appeared at the hottest part of the day—early afternoon—when people usually rested and ate the main meal of the day. Abraham himself was resting, and he invited the strangers to stop and refresh themselves before they continued on their way. **What details reveal Abraham's spirit of hospitality? What did he do when he saw the three men? What was his tone of voice? How did he refer to himself in relationship to them? Do we have any indication that Abraham knew it was the Lord himself?** Use these questions to help your group see the spirit of welcome, generosity, and respect that Abraham held toward others.

   The expression "if I have found favor in your eyes" (v. 3) was commonly used by someone extending an invitation to a person of higher rank. "My lord" also suggests reverence and respect. Abraham probably did not know at that point that he was actually speaking to the Lord; only later do we learn that the two who accompanied the Lord were angels (19:1).

2. *Genesis 18:6-12*

   a. *How did Abraham and Sarah provide for the visitors?*
   b. *What was the purpose of this visit?*
   c. *How did Sarah respond to the Lord's statement? Why?*

**What details in this passage give more evidence of Abraham's spirit of hospitality?** Your group should note that Abraham, though an old man of one hundred years, "hurried" into the tent and told Sarah to make some bread—"Quick!" Then he "ran" to the herd and selected the calf himself. The servant "hurried" to prepare the meal. The three seahs of fine flour Abraham ordered (v. 6) was about twenty quarts, a huge quantity of flour for just three men. And, though it was the custom for the host to dine with his guests, Abraham stood respectfully to the side while the three men ate.

During the conversation that followed the meal, Abraham and Sarah learned that their visitors were indeed out of the ordinary. They knew more than mere humans would know. **Why might the Lord have chosen to visit Abraham again in this way? Of what did he want to reassure Abraham? Why might he have specifically asked about Sarah?** It seems that God wanted to reaffirm again to Abraham and Sarah that, in spite of the seeming impossibility, God would give them a child.

As Abraham had laughed previously, so Sarah now laughed. **What was she questioning? Might it have been a different kind of laughter from Abraham's?** Apparently she was past menopause (v. 11), being ninety years old. Though the Scripture does not specify the cause of Sarah's laughter, it is possible that Sarah's laughter came from a spirit of mockery and disbelief.

3. *Genesis 18:13-15*

   a. *How did the Lord respond to Sarah?*
   b. *What did Sarah say to the Lord? Why?*

Verse 14 contains a rhetorical question: "Is anything too hard for the Lord?" Explore the meaning of this question. **Do they believe that there is nothing too hard for the Lord? What did this mean for Abraham and Sarah? What does it mean for believers today? What does this tell us about the nature of God? Do you think it means that God will do everything just because he is able to do it? Why or why not?** Your discussion should emphasize the importance of knowing not only God's power (his ability to do anything) but also his character, since God does only those things that reveal his character of love, justice, mercy, holiness, and so on. God may be able to do anything, but he will not do those things that go against his nature.

Your group might also appreciate this honest glimpse into Sarah's human nature. **Who would not be afraid to tell God that they had laughed at his promise?** Sarah's response was all too human. **Did God condemn**
38

her? Or did he merely ask her—gently—to face the truth about herself? What does this tell us about God—and about our fears of letting God know the truth about ourselves?

4. *Genesis 18:16-19*

   a. *What promise did the Lord repeat here?*

   b. *What responsibilities did Abraham carry as the head of his household?*

In this passage we learn that God's covenant with Abraham means that his descendants are expected to follow God's law and to do what is right and just. **What do we learn about God? How does he treat people? How is this consistent with what we've learned so far about God in Genesis?**

Some of your group members may have difficulty with the idea that God chose Abraham (v. 19). Help them to remember the beginning of Abraham's story, where the Lord called Abraham out of Haran and offered to be a God to him and his family. **Who was responsible for initiating and maintaining the covenant recorded in Genesis 15? Who "owned" the covenant?**

5. *Genesis 18:20-21*

   *Why did the Lord want to visit Sodom and Gomorrah?*

The story of these two cities has become a symbol of God's justice and his anger at human wickedness. In a sense, the Lord was here beginning legal proceedings against these two cities. He planned to visit these cities to get an eyewitness account of their wickedness, to see for himself the evil that had caused its victims to cry out to God. **How is this different from the view of God as someone who sits high above the heavens without getting personally involved in human history, blindly pulling the strings of fate?**

Explore the idea of God as a fair judge. **What does verse 19 tell us about God's standards? How previously has God showed himself as a just judge?** In his prayer for Sodom and Gomorrah, Abraham was allowed to become a partner with God, arguing on behalf of others.

**What exactly may have been the "outcry" mentioned in verses 20-21?** The Hebrew word in verse 20 suggests a sense of outrage, a plea for help from oppression. The word for "outcry" in verse 22 is similar to that used in the story of Abel's murder, when his blood cried out to God from the ground. **How might the situation in Sodom and Gomorrah have been similar to what happened between Cain and Abel? Who may have been crying out to the Lord for justice?** Though the verse does not specify this, we can assume that the victims of these cities' wickedness must have prayed for relief and justice.

This is the first time that the theme of justice versus oppression occurs in the Bible, a theme often repeated throughout the Old and New Testaments. **What does this passage tell us about God's concern for victims of**

**oppression and wickedness?** The Lord hears and investigates the cries for help from those who suffer injustice. **Did the Lord have to go down to these cities in order to know what was going on? What does his investigation of the situation tell us about God?** You may find it helpful to look up the following passages that refer to the sin of Sodom and Gomorrah: Genesis 13:13; 19:5; Jeremiah 23:14; and Ezekiel 16:49-50. These tell us that these cities' sins included sexual perversion, indifference to the poor, social oppression, adultery, lying, and encouraging evildoers.

6. *Genesis 18:22-26*
   a. *What was Abraham's line of reasoning with God?*
   b. *On what did he base his argument?*

Notice that Abraham did not intercede for Lot by name but for a group of righteous people. **Why did Abraham bargain with the Lord for the welfare of Sodom and Gomorrah? How is his prayer for these cities a concrete example of his being a blessing to the nations?** Abraham explored the scope of God's judgment and mercy as he questioned how much value God places on the righteousness of a small group of people. He wanted to know what carried more weight with God—the sin of many or the righteousness of a few. Abraham focused on the issue of innocence and guilt, as well as on the issue of looking at the community as a whole rather than at isolated individuals.

**What basic assumption lies behind Abraham's argument?** Abraham assumed that the Lord acts responsibly and in a way that humans can understand.

7. *Genesis 18:27-33*
   a. *How did Abraham describe himself to the Lord?*
   b. *How far did Abraham go in his bargaining with the Lord?*
   c. *How did the Lord respond to Abraham's requests?*
   d. *How does this episode end?*

Group members may not have noticed in their reading that Abraham addressed God by the formal title of "Lord" (indicated in the NIV by lowercase letters) rather than the more intimate Hebrew word for "LORD" (indicated in the NIV by uppercase letters). He was appealing to the Lord in his more formal role as judge of all the earth. **Was the Lord being just? Would it be just to destroy the righteous with the wicked?** (Grow groups may want to discuss the truth that the presence of a few righteous can save others from destruction; see also Gen. 39:5; Matt. 13:24-30; and Acts 27:24.) If your group has studied Genesis 1-11, you might ask how this situation was similar to that at the time of Noah.

Why Abraham stopped his pleading with God at the number ten remains a mystery. Perhaps ten was the smallest number that could be considered a group or community (in later times, for example, ten men were needed to form a Jewish synagogue).

8. *Genesis 18:1-33*

   a. *What new things do we learn from this passage about God's dealings with people?*

   b. *How would you describe the God portrayed in this chapter?*

Studying these two stories should enrich your group's understanding of how the Lord deals with two different kinds of people. On the one hand, he responds to evil by coming to judge for himself the truth of the situation. On the other hand, he is ready to save even the most wicked culture for the sake of a handful of righteous. This theme is echoed in Jesus' words on salt and light in Matthew 5:13-16.

Listen sensitively as group members share their perceptions of God. Some may see God as personal and caring, others as judgmental and harsh. Be ready to follow through with members who may be earnestly searching to know God or who need reassurance.

# Lesson 7

Genesis 19:1-38

# The Just God

## Introductory Notes

As you begin this lesson, be sure to review Lot's history. **How was he related to Abraham? How did he arrive at Sodom? What do we already know about Sodom? What direction does Lot's life seem to have taken? How might these things have removed Lot from consideration as Abraham's heir?** If your group has already studied Genesis 1-11, make sure they are aware of the similarities between Lot's situation and Noah's.

## Optional Opening Share Question

**Do you find it easy to wait? Why?**

1. *Genesis 19:1-3*

   *What do these verses tell us about Lot?*

   The angels met Lot in the gateway of the city—a place that served as the community center for transacting legal and business affairs. Lot's presence there indicates that he may have become a member of the ruling council. It was also common for travelers to roll themselves in their cloaks and sleep in the large city square.

   **How did Lot greet the strangers? Why do you think he was so insistent that they come home with him? What was his concern?** Lot's welcome of the two men was certainly hospitable, similar to his uncle Abraham's—but his words and actions convey a feeling of alarm and anxiety. Even the meal he prepared was hasty; bread without yeast could be made in a hurry. Though he probably did not know at this point that these two men were angels, he seems to have been well aware of the dangers that travelers faced in this wicked city.

2. *Genesis 19:4-8*

   a. *What kind of crowd gathered in front of Lot's house? What did they demand?*

   b. *How did Lot reply? Why might he have said this?*

   Lot's offering his daughters to the mob may seem peculiar to your group. However, the way in which he offered them implies that he did not expect

43

the offer to be accepted. Perhaps the strong Mideastern emphasis on hospitality made Lot more concerned about protecting his guests than his daughters, especially in a culture where men were considered more important than women.

Acknowledge the feelings of outrage your group members will undoubtedly have at this point. Ask if they can now more clearly understand the cry for justice mentioned earlier. **How does this incident help us understand God's desire to destroy this city?** Some members may point out that the permissiveness in today's society is dangerously close to Sodom's. Give your group members the freedom to vent their feelings about this passage. Don't feel as though you have to provide answers; just try to keep from getting sidetracked.

3. *Genesis 19:9-11*

   a. *What did the crowd say about Lot?*

   b. *How did the angels help Lot? What does this reveal about them?*

**How did Lot address the crowd (v. 6)?** His calling them "friends" suggests that he considered himself somewhat of an equal among the people of his community. **Did the men of the city seem to agree with this? What do their comments tell us about Lot? About the men of the city themselves?** The crowd's reply shows that the people of Sodom saw Lot as a stranger and an outsider—and so without authority. Typical of a mob, they used their own logic to justify getting what they wanted.

The men's refusal to accept Lot as their judge suggests that perhaps Lot had been pointing out their wrongs for a long time. This is only a hint, however; it may also have been that Lot's more upright lifestyle had condemned his neighbors without Lot's having had to say a word.

The word for *blindness* here is not the Hebrew word commonly used to indicate sightlessness; rather, it indicates a temporary, dazzled state— perhaps caused by supernatural conditions (see also 2 Kings 6:18). It is ironic that Lot, who had gone out to protect the strangers, ended up having to be protected by them. **What did Lot learn about the strangers at this point?**

4. *Genesis 19:12-14*

   a. *What did the two men tell Lot to do?*

   b. *What reasons did they give for their advice?*

Remind your group that the Lord had said that he was going to investigate the sin of Sodom and Gomorrah before passing judgment on these two cities (18:20-21). **What had the two angels learned about the men of Sodom? How had the city's guilt been established?** The rest of this story deals with the resulting judgment on the two cities. Explore the ways in which the Lord had been patient with Sodom. **On what was his patience based? Had Abraham's concerns regarding the Lord's mercy and justice been satisfied?**

Some in your group may question why the two angels made such an effort to save Lot and his family. **Is there much evidence that Lot was still a righteous man?** From his treatment of the two strangers, we can assume that Lot was still somewhat of a God-fearing man, given to hospitality and concerned with others. Yet he had settled in a city of great wickedness, and his children were intermarrying with the people there. Evidently he was a property owner and a ruler in the town. **How may his character have been affected by this? How did he differ from Abraham in this regard?** God saved Lot, much as he had saved Noah before; but Noah was a righteous man, and God had rescued him and his family for Noah's sake. **But what does verse 29 suggest about God's rescue of Lot? Whom was God remembering when he did this?** Moreover, in contrast to Noah's family, Lot's sons-in-law did not seem at all eager to take advantage of this offer of salvation.

5. *Genesis 19:15-22*

   a. *Why did the angels continue to urge Lot?*

   b. *What did Lot ask of the angels? Why did he ask it?*

   c. *How did Lot's response to the angels differ from the response of his sons-in-law?*

   d. *What did the angel promise to do when Lot reached Zoar?*

Note the sense of urgency in the angels' words. **How many times does the word** *flee* **occur in this passage?** Note also that they had to physically push Lot and his family out of the city. The angels urged haste, telling Lot and his family not to look back on pain of death. Apparently the angels could not act until they knew that Lot was safely out of harm's way (v. 22). Note God's patience. **Why might God have been so patient with Lot?** In contrast to Abraham and Noah, Lot hesitated to obey God's commands. **What does this tell us about the importance Lot placed on his material possessions and on the status he was leaving behind?**

Look also at Lot's request to stay in the town of Zoar. **Why might he have wanted to do this? What does his desire to stay in the plains tell us about the importance of his original decision to settle there? Might he have been thinking of his original agreement with Abraham? Might he have been reluctant to face the more difficult life in the dry, rugged mountains (v. 19)?**

6. *Genesis 19:23-29*

   a. *What happened to the two cities?*

   b. *Why did God save Lot?*

Although the precise location of Sodom is not known, scholars suggest that the shallow end of the Dead Sea was once the valley of Siddem, where Sodom was located. The description of the destruction of Sodom reminds us of an earthquake with sulfurous fire. The "fire and brimstone" imagery has become a symbol for God's judgment throughout the Old Testament. The word *overthrew* (v. 25) is the word used to indicate great catastrophe in the Scriptures; it means literally "to turn upside down." (See also Luke 17:26-35.)

However, God's judgment can be postponed or turned aside by the presence of righteous people. **How did Abraham stand between God's judgment and the people of Sodom? How did God answer Abraham's bargaining in Genesis 18?**

7. *Genesis 19:30-35*

   a. *What was Lot's situation after Sodom was destroyed?*

   b. *What did his daughters do? Why?*

**Why might Lot have moved from Zoar? What might he have feared?** The text does not explain why Lot was afraid; perhaps he did not trust God to protect him if he stayed in the city (see v. 17). So he went to the mountains after all, as the angels had told him to.

Life in the cave must have been difficult; it was certainly lonely. Lot's existence there was a high price to pay for his earlier greed and poor judgment in settling on the plain. Lot's two daughters apparently had no contact with other people, and they realized that it would be impossible for them to marry and have children. The culture of that day placed great importance on carrying on the family line. **How did Lot's daughters propose to solve this problem? What is the crucial difference between the ending of this story and that of Sarah's barrenness?** The Lord's presence and covenant faithfulness is very evident in the life of Sarah and Abraham; but Lot and his daughters, having chosen to live in a culture that rejected God's laws, were left to their own devices. It's important, however, to realize that the two daughters were motivated not so much by lust as by a desire to continue the family line.

If your group has studied Genesis 1-11, note the echoes of the story of Noah's drunkenness. **What came of each man's drunken state? How were the children involved?**

8. *Genesis 19:36-38*

   *What happened as a result of the two daughters' actions?*

Although the family line continued, Lot and his descendants had removed themselves from inclusion in Abraham's family. **What two tribes descended from the incest between Lot and his daughters?** The Ammonites and Moabites eventually settled in the desert on Israel's eastern border. They became bitter enemies of Israel (see, for example, 1 Sam. 14:47 and 2 Chron. 20:1). However, the Israelites always remembered that they were "brothers" to these tribes, especially when God prohibited Israel from occupying the land of the Ammonites and Moabites when they entered Canaan, explaining that he had given those territories to the descendants of Lot (Deut. 2:9, 19).

9. *Genesis 19:1-38*

   *In what ways had the Lord shown himself to be both a just and merciful God?*

Two themes should be part of your summary discussion: God's justice and the contrast between Abraham and Lot. As you discuss God's justice, ask some of the following questions: **On what is God's justice based? What happened when Abraham bargained with the Lord about the fate of Sodom? How had the Lord been just to both Sodom and Lot? How did his justice include mercy?**

Lot and Abraham's lifestyles were very different. Mention some of the following contrasts: Abraham's free and hospitable hosting of his visitors and Lot's fearfully hiding them from his neighbors; Abraham's assurance of God's blessing on his home and land and Lot's living in continual danger and having to flee for his life; Lot's pleading for himself, not for the city, and Abraham's pleading for Lot and for Sodom, but not for himself. **What do these contrasts suggest about the future of these two men?**

# Lesson 8

Genesis 20:1–21:7

## Promises Fulfilled

### Introductory Comments

This story is similar to that of Abraham's earlier visit to Egypt (Gen. 12:10-20). Be sure to review that story with your group as you begin to study this passage. Use the suggested supplementary questions to help your group compare the two.

You should also compare this story with the destruction of Sodom, talking about God's justice and his dealings with those outside the household of Abraham. Again, use the suggested supplementary questions to help your group explore these issues.

### Optional Opening Share Question

**What makes you laugh?**

1. *Genesis 20:1-3*

   a. *What happened to Abraham and Sarah when they moved to Gerar?*

   b. *What did God say to Abimelech?*

The story does not tell us why Abimelech took Sarah to be his wife. **What was Pharaoh's reason for taking Sarah in Abraham's earlier visit to Egypt? How old was Sarah now? Would her beauty still have been outstanding?** Though Sarah may still have been beautiful enough to have attracted Abimelech's eye, it is more likely that Abimelech wanted to cement his relationship with this powerful, wandering chieftain by marrying the woman whom he thought was Abraham's sister—a common custom in that day.

Perhaps the point of the story, however, is this: Abraham needed to realize that he could find God-fearing people among the surrounding nations. **What had been Abraham's experience with the people of Sodom? How might this have influenced his perspective on the other nations around him?** The fact that God could not find even ten righteous people in the city of Sodom must have been discouraging to Abraham, who had pleaded with God to spare the city. Now he had to learn the opposite lesson: among the world's cultures not all were like Sodom. **In light of the story of Abraham in Egypt, what do we know about Abraham's fears in the land of Gerar? How did Abraham deal with these fears? What was missing** from Abraham's plan of action? In what way was Abraham again less than a blessing to the nations here?

Look also at the possible consequences of Abraham's actions. **What might be some of the results of his decision? Whom was God protecting when he appeared to Abimelech? Why might he have warned Abimelech directly?** Note that God was protecting Abraham and Sarah, and also Abimelech, who had not acted with evil intent toward God's chosen people.

2.  *Genesis 20:4-7*

    a.  *How did Abimelech respond to God's warning?*

    b.  *How had Sarah been kept safe?*

    c.  *What choices did the Lord give Abimelech?*

    d.  *What might Abimelech have learned about God from this incident?*

Your group may notice a similarity between Abraham and Abimelech: both pleaded with God for justice (see Gen. 18:23-25). **What did both men believe about God? What did they assume about God's nature?** Both Abraham and Abimelech were confident of the Lord's ability to judge justly. Abimelech found himself in a kind of legal defense, arguing to change the death penalty that God had brought against him. He based his argument on the purity of his motives toward Sarah. He apparently was fully aware that taking a married woman to be his wife was a sin. He did not try to cover up his action; rather, he honestly explained his mistake and tried to deal with the situation justly. **How did this contrast with Abraham's actions?**

As you discuss verses 6-7, ask your group whom God was really trying to protect here. **What does this tell us about Sarah's value in God's eyes? What might this have to do with the promise God gave to Sarah (18:13-14)? Again, how does God's concern contrast with Abraham's actions?** Set between the promise of a son to Sarah and the birth of Isaac, God's warning was meant to protect Sarah before the birth of her son.

The word *prophet* (v. 7) appears here for the first time in the Old Testament. Since newcomer groups will be unfamiliar with the Old Testament prophets, you may want to explain that a prophet was someone God used to speak his words to people; a prophet served as God's mouthpiece. A prophet also had the privilege of speaking to God on behalf of other people. **How did Abraham assume the prophet's role? In what ways had he served as God's prophet before?**

3.  *Genesis 20:8-13*

    a.  *Who was at fault here, according to Abimelech?*

    b.  *How did Abraham try to justify his actions? How many of his statements are true?*

The conversation between Abraham and Abimelech also deals with accusations and defense. This time Abraham was on the defensive, and he was found guilty. He acknowledged his guilt by his double-talk and weak excuses. In fact, he sounds much like Adam responding to God in the Garden of Eden. In effect, he told Abimelech that he had not expected to find basic human kindness and respect in any foreign country. **How was Abraham proved wrong? Who had shown greater fear of God in this case—Abraham or Abimelech?**

Abraham also had to learn that the Lord used this fear of God among the heathens to protect Abraham and his family. This incident with Abimelech showed how much Abraham's fear was misplaced. **In what way does this episode soften what Abraham had learned about the wickedness of Sodom?**

4. *Genesis 20:14-18*

    *a.  How did Abimelech make up for the injustice to Sarah?*

    *b.  What did the Lord do for Abimelech's family? Through what means?*

The author here seems mostly concerned with vindicating Sarah, showing that she was blameless and that Abimelech paid handsomely for any wrong he had done to her. The money Abimelech publicly presented to her was a sign to all who saw it that Sarah had no blame in the matter. She had remained pure. Abimelech also gave Abraham great wealth in livestock and slaves. **How does his behavior contrast with the way Abraham had behaved throughout this whole episode? Who showed more concern for Sarah? More fear of God?**

Contrast this story with that of Abraham in Egypt (12:10-20). **How did Abimelech treat Abraham differently than Pharaoh did? What might have made the difference?** Abimelech graciously allowed Abraham to move freely throughout the land, whereas Pharaoh had sent Abraham quickly out of Egypt. Abimelech also gave Abraham much wealth after he learned that Sarah was Abraham's wife, whereas Pharaoh had paid Abraham before he took Sarah to be his wife. No doubt, Abimelech was more of a God-fearing man than Pharaoh was, as his conversation with God suggests.

Ironically, Abimelech's household suffered from the same condition—barrenness—that Sarah did. Apparently Abimelech was included in some way in this punishment, though the Scripture does not specify his ailment. **Why might the Lord have chosen this kind of disease to afflict Abimelech and his household?** Perhaps it kept Abimelech away from Sarah (see v. 6).

Note the role of prayer in this story. **What do we learn about the importance of prayer? Why might the Lord have used this method of healing Abimelech and his household? What would this have taught both Abraham and Abimelech?**

5. *Genesis 21:1-7*

   a. *How did God fulfill his promise to Sarah?*
   b. *What is significant about Isaac's circumcision?*
   c. *Why was the baby given the name Isaac?*
   d. *How was this name fitting, given the circumstances of Isaac's conception and birth?*

Abraham's history climaxes with the arrival of his long-awaited son. Remind your group that Isaac's name means "he laughs." **How did Sarah tie this in with the birth? How is it connected with Genesis 17:17 and 18:12? In what way can we say the Lord had the "last laugh"? What kind of laughter was Sarah talking about?** Laughter often accompanies joy. This occasion—the fulfillment of God's promises—surely was one of great joy. **How did Sarah reflect the wonder of what had happened to her and Abraham? What does it mean that the Lord was "gracious" to Sarah? What does this tell us about God?**

Note with your group that Isaac was the first person in the Bible to be circumcised as an infant on the eighth day, as the Lord had commanded. **How was this different from Ishmael? How does this reinforce the surety of Isaac's place as the promised son?**

6. *Genesis 20:1–21:7*

   *How did the Lord keep his promises to Abraham and Sarah, according to this passage?*

Summarize the theme of promise and delay in the lives of Abraham and Sarah. **What promises had God made to them? In what ways were they made to wait? What does this tell us about the way God may fulfill some of his promises?** (Grow groups may want to discuss times in which the fulfillment of God's promises seemed to be delayed in their own lives.) As you reflect together, be sensitive to those who may be struggling to have faith in God's promises or who have become discouraged because such promises have been delayed. **What does the story of Abraham have to say to people today?**

# Lesson 9

Genesis 21:8-34; 25:12-18

# The Second Son

## Introductory Notes

This lesson continues the story of Hagar and Ishmael that began in Genesis 16. **What did we learn about the relationship between Hagar and Sarah? What did Hagar do as a result? How did the Lord respond to her troubles? What did he promise her concerning Ishmael?** Use these questions to review that story, since the passage for this lesson presents the sequel. Ishmael was permanently banished from Abraham's family; he no longer had any claim to Isaac's inheritance. Although Hagar and Ishmael were sent away, God did not forget them. He continued to watch over the two outcasts. If your group has previously studied Genesis 1-11, you may want to compare the fate of Hagar and Ishmael with that of Cain (Gen. 4).

## Optional Opening Share Question

**Does your name have a meaning? What is it?**

1. *Genesis 21:8-10*
    a. *What tension was building in the relationships in Abraham's family?*
    b. *What was the history of this tension?*

Though many translations use the word *mocking* (v. 9), the original meaning may have been simply "at play." Whatever the case, this incident was used to separate Ishamael and Isaac. **Why might Sarah in particular have felt this was necessary? What threat did she feel? Why?** As the eldest son, Ishmael would have been the logical choice as the heir of Abraham's estate. Ishmael's continued presence worried Sarah; she wanted him officially disinherited.

Sarah's request to Abraham suggests that Hagar would receive her freedom in exchange for her son's claim to the inheritance. To accomplish this, Abraham would have to transfer his responsibility for Ishmael to Hagar. **Why would this be necessary?** The legal codes of that day give us some insight into the situation. Legally, when a wife gave her handmaid to her husband in order to produce an heir, the handmaid's child became the legal heir and belonged to the husband and his wife. But if they decided to disinherit that child for any reason, the child and his mother would be freed.

Evidently Abraham had hesitated to do this, although he knew that Isaac would be his heir. Perhaps he had been torn by his love for his firstborn son.

2. *Genesis 21:11-14*

   a. *What was Abraham's response to Sarah's demand?*
   b. *Why did the Lord tell Abraham to listen to Sarah?*

Since releasing Hagar and Ishmael was part of the legal procedure for disinheritance, the Lord told Abraham to do what Sarah had demanded. **What might have been the Lord's reasons for doing this?** Two reasons come to mind: first, the promise was to Isaac as the promised son. Second, God had also promised that he would continue to protect Ishmael and make him a great nation. Abraham could be assured that he was not sending Hagar and Ishmael to their death; God would be with them.

So Abraham gave Ishmael up to his mother and sent them off. Once again, the biblical account narrows its focus to only one family, one line— the people of promise. **In what way might this separation have been another test of Abraham's faith?** Abraham's sole hope now lay in Isaac—a truth that we will explore in the next lesson. For now, help your group to see that Abraham had to believe completely that the Lord would fulfill his promise through only one son.

Ishmael was no longer a boy at this point; he must have been between fifteen and eighteen years of age. Provided with food and water, he and his mother wandered off into the desert. **How did this begin to fulfill the Lord's word to Hagar (Gen. 16:12)?**

Ishmael's banishment may seem cruel to your group. If they have studied Genesis 1-11, they may be reminded of Adam being banished from Eden, of Cain being banished to wander the earth, and of the people of Babel being dispersed throughout the world. **How did each of these instances serve the Lord's purpose for his world? How did the separation between Isaac and Ishmael do the same?** (Read Gal. 4:21-31 for a New Testament perspective on this story.)

3. *Genesis 21:15-19*

   a. *In what situation did Hagar find herself?*
   b. *Who spoke to her?*
   c. *What promise did God make regarding Ishmael's future?*
   d. *What did God do for Hagar to assure her that he would keep his promises of care and blessing?*
   e. *What continuing pattern of God's care do we see here and throughout the story of Abraham?*

Once again the meaning of Ishmael's name ("God hears") is emphasized (v. 17). **To whom had God promised earlier that Ishmael would become a great nation (17:20; 21:13)? To whom did God restate this promise?** Look back to the promises God had made concerning Ishmael (including 16:10-12). **How are these promises similar to those made regarding Isaac? How are they different?** Note that the promise of land and the call to a special relationship with the Lord are missing. **Why might this be so?**

The expression "God opened her eyes" suggests that the well had always been there, but that for some reason Hagar had been kept from seeing it. Grow groups may want to discuss how Hagar's experience of God's care is similar to the experiences of people today. **How might God open our eyes in a time of need to a "well of water" that we couldn't see before, though it may have been there all the time? What do these experiences tell us about God?**

4. *Genesis 21:20-21; 25:12-18*

   *Note that these two Scripture passages are taken from separate chapters in Genesis. The excerpt from chapter 25 is included to finish the account of Ishmael's history.*

   a. *What became of Ishmael?*

   b. *How did his descendants reflect Ishmael's nature?*

**How was Ishmael's life different from Isaac's?** The desert was home to Ishmael, while Isaac lived in the cultivated and civilized land of Canaan. Ishmael took an Egyptian wife and became a hunter with weapons; whereas Isaac remained with his parents and, we assume, was brought up to care for the many flocks and herds owned by his father.

Though there is no genealogy in the Bible that begins with Abraham's name, both of his sons are given their own genealogy. Scholars speculate that Ishmael's descendants occupied the territory of the Arabian peninsula. (You may want to point out on a map this land that lay between Canaan and Egypt.) So they remained near Abraham's family, but their territory had distinct borders. Ishmael's genealogy shows that the Lord fulfilled his promises regarding this son of Abraham. However, the genealogy is short, suggesting that we are to dismiss this family line and get on with the main story—that of Abraham and the son of promise.

5. *Genesis 21:22-24*

   a. *What did Abimelech recognize about Abraham?*

   b. *What was Abimelech's concern in his relationship with Abraham?*

Once again we see Abraham in a broader context, relating to the people among whom he lived. **What does your group remember about Abimelech? What kind of person was he? How had Abraham dealt with** him? Note that the two leaders treated each other as equals; they respected and trusted each other. But Abimelech recognized that God had given Abraham special treatment. **How do his words reflect some fulfillment already of God's promises to Abraham?**

**Why was Abimelech concerned about his descendants? Why might this story have been told after the story of Isaac's birth?** Your group should see that Abimelech was concerned that Abraham's descendants not try to dominate or fight against his own descendants, especially since he saw that God was with this special family. **Did Abraham respond to Abimelech's concern?**

6. *Genesis 21:25-30*

   a. *What complaint did Abraham bring to Abimelech?*

   b. *How did the two settle the dispute?*

There is an abrupt break between verses 24 and 25. After the treaty between Abraham and Abimelech, the king's servants seized a well that Abraham had dug. In the culture of that time, the person who dug a well owned it. The water rights were vital to the survival of extensive flocks and herds.

So Abraham and Abimelech made another treaty to formally acknowledge Abraham's right of ownership to the well. It was customary to seal such covenants with blood, so Abraham may have given the sheep and cattle with this purpose in mind. In accepting these animals, Abimelech was affirming that Abraham had a right to claim the well.

7. *Genesis 21:31-34*

   a. *Why was the place named Beersheba?*

   b. *What did Abraham do after the treaty had been made? What does this tell us about him?*

Note the name used for God here—*El Olam*—"the Everlasting God." In other words, Abraham acknowledged God as the Eternal One, the God who is from everlasting to everlasting. He called on this unchanging God to witness the covenant between him and Abimelech. The NIV footnote tells us that *Beersheba* can mean either "well of the oath" or "well of seven," referring perhaps to the custom of repeating an oath seven times. Abraham planted a tamarisk tree as a memorial—a fitting tree to plant, since the tamarisk is noted for its long life. **What might be the author's reason for including this incident in Abraham's history? What does it tell us about Abraham's relationship to God? In what ways was Abraham here a witness to others about his God?**

The final verse of this passage reminds us that Abraham was still in the land of the Philistines. **What is significant about this?** In spite of having dug wells and claimed ownership in some sense, Abraham was still a wanderer, living as an "alien" (v. 23) in a land that did not belong to him.

8. *Genesis 21:8-34; 25:12-18*

   *In what ways did God continue to be faithful to Abraham, according to these passages?*

As you summarize this lesson, focus on God's care for the people associated with Abraham. **Why did God remain concerned with Hagar and Ishmael? In what way was Abraham a blessing to the nations?**

# Lesson 10

Genesis 22:1-19

# The Sacrifice

## Introductory Notes

This passage relates the ultimate test of Abraham's faith in God's ability to keep his promises. As you begin, review some of the previous tests of Abraham's faith. **What promises had God made to him? What stood in the way of those promises? How had Abraham responded to those tests? How had God provided for him?**

This test was the most severe, however. Isaac was the son of promise. What would happen if that son were killed? As your group will see early in the lesson, God was asking Abraham to cut himself off from his future in the same way that he had asked Abraham earlier to cut himself off from his past (Gen. 12).

As you discuss this passage, be prepared to answer questions about why God tests people. **What is a test of one's faith? How does it differ from temptation? What might God be trying to prove? For whose benefit might this test have been conducted?** If you think the group will find it helpful, refer to the story of Job (Job 1:1-12) when these questions arise.

## Optional Opening Share Question

**Is there anyone you would trust no matter what they told you to do?**

1. *Genesis 22:1-2*
    a. *How did God test Abraham?*
    b. *From what we know of Abraham, why would this have been an especially difficult test?*

Your group may be shocked at God's request for a human sacrifice. Explain that such sacrifices were common in the pagan religions of Abraham's time, although there is no record in Scripture that God ever required human sacrifice (except for Jesus, who was also a well-loved and only Son). Animal sacrifices were part of the worship of the one true God (Abel and Noah both offered such sacrifices to God). **How did God's words to Abraham emphasize the severity of this test?** The repetition of "your only son . . . whom you love" reveals God's awareness that Abraham loved his son deeply. Remind your group that God had asked Abraham earlier to leave behind his past—his relatives, his family history, his cultural roots—and go to the land of Canaan. **Now what was God asking him to give up?** God was asking Abraham to give up his future, to sacrifice his only hope for a family through Sarah and Isaac. **Why was this such a difficult test for Abraham? Why might God have asked it of him at this point in his life?** Explore with your group God's desire that Abraham trust in God wholly, obeying him above all else. **What does this tell us about the covenant God had made with Abraham? What did God expect of his covenant people? Had Abraham always shown perfect trust in God?** As you discuss some of Abraham's earlier decisions, your group should see that God had reason to test Abraham's faith—especially now that he had the precious son of the promise.

**What do Abraham's words (v. 1) tell us about his relationship with God?** "Here I am" is the response of a servant ready to do his master's will. **What hint do these words give as to how Abraham would respond to God's command?**

Moriah was about a three-day journey from the area where Abraham was living. He would have to make preparations for such a long trip there and back. Though God does not specify the exact location in this passage, 2 Chronicles 3:1 identifies the place of sacrifice as Mount Moriah, the mountain on which the temple in Jerusalem is located.

2. *Genesis 22:3-8*

   a. *What preparations did Abraham make in response to God's command?*

   b. *How did Abraham answer Isaac's question? What did he mean?*

   c. *What do these verses tell us about Abraham's faith? In what ways had it matured?*

Note the speed of Abraham's response: "Early the next morning . . ." **What must Abraham have felt about God's request? What thoughts and questions might have been going through his mind? Yet how did he respond to God's command?** Your group should see Abraham's complete and prompt obedience, in spite of the agony he must have wrestled with during the night. Encourage your group to imagine themselves in Abraham's place so that they have a better understanding of the struggle he faced in this test. **How does Abraham's response contrast with Lot's response to God's command (Gen. 19:15-20)? How might you account for this difference?**

**What might have enabled Abraham to obey God as he did?** Look at Abraham's words in these verses, especially verses 5 and 8: "*We* will come back to you"; "God himself will provide the lamb." **What did Abraham know about God by this time?** Center your discussion on the evidences of God's faithfulness, his power, and his just dealings with people. **Had Abraham experienced all of these firsthand? When?**

Abraham's reply to Isaac was more evasive than literal. He really did not know what would happen or how the Lord would provide. A more accurate translation of these words is, "God will see for himself." **What kind of ending to the story might we anticipate, given these words?**

3. *Genesis 22:9-10*
   a. *What final preparations did Abraham make?*
   b. *In what ways did he show his faithfulness to God?*

"The place God had told him about" (v. 9) refers back to verse 3. Note with your group that the story slows down at this point, recording each move with care. **What might be the reason for this? What do these details tell us about Abraham?** Encourage your group to put themselves in Abraham's place emotionally. **How must he have felt as he bound Isaac with ropes? As he laid him on the altar? As he poised the knife above him?** Note also Isaac's obedient submission. He was old enough to have climbed the mountain with his father and strong enough to have helped carry the wood and provisions. Surely he could have resisted as his aged father tied him with ropes and placed him on the altar. **What does this tell us about Isaac?**

The drama of this moment can hardly be equaled in all of Scripture. What will happen to this obedient man and his son?

4. *Genesis 22:11-12*
   a. *What stopped Abraham from sacrificing Isaac?*
   b. *According to the angel, how had Abraham demonstrated his fear of God?*

At the last possible minute, the angel stopped Abraham's hand. **Why might he have waited so long to interfere?** Abraham learned that the test was given to prove his willingness to obey the Lord in spite of apparent inconsistencies in the Lord's word. Be sure that your group members understand that God knows all things; he knew that Abraham's faith would prove genuine and obedient. Perhaps the test was more for Abraham's benefit—to test the depth of his commitment to God. This helps us understand God's purpose in testing believers: to confirm their faith and to prove their commitment. See Luke 18:18-30 and James 1:2-4 to expand on this idea.

God repeated Abraham's name to emphasize the urgency of his message. **In what other ways do his words indicate the enormity of what Abraham was about to do?** The phrase "now I know" (usually used in the Bible by people who have seen God act on their behalf) is here used by God to indicate the depth of his certainty about Abraham's heart. **What does it mean to "fear God"?** As you talk about this phrase, your group should come to identify it with Abraham's obedience to God's commands and his acknowledgment of God's total claim on his life.

5. *Genesis 22:13-14*

   a. *How was Isaac replaced as the sacrifice?*
   b. *What is the significance of the name Abraham gave that place?*

The text does not indicate how or when the ram had gotten caught in the bushes, but we do know that Abraham named that place "The Lord Will Provide." **What does this tell us about who provided the ram? What does this name have to do with Abraham's words to Isaac in verse 8?** The ram died in place of Isaac, one of the first recorded instances where an animal was substituted for a human in a sacrifice. **What other biblical examples of this can you think of?** Use Isaiah 53:4-9 to relate this concept to Jesus' death. Jesus is often referred to as "the Lamb of God," the One who was provided by God to die in our place. The ram that God provided for Abraham foreshadowed the sacrifice God would provide for all of Abraham's spiritual descendants. Be sensitive to the opportunity to present the gospel here. The Holy Spirit may use this lesson to open someone's heart to the meaning of Christ's death in his or her place.

6. *Genesis 22:15-19*

   a. *What would be the result of Abraham's obedience?*
   b. *What new promise is included in God's list of blessings?*

This is the last conversation the Bible records between God and Abraham. **How did the Lord express his commitment to Abraham here? Why might the Lord have sworn this promise in his own name ("I swear by myself," v. 15)?** The Lord swore by himself because there was no one higher than him; no one else could act as a righteous judge to see that the oath was carried out. This is the only time Genesis records that God swore this kind of oath, which indicates the depth of the Lord's commitment to Abraham.

God's promises to Abraham, coming as they do after the ultimate test of Abraham's commitment, become part of the final chapter on the development of Abraham's faith. Notice that God's last word to him is that he will become a blessing to all nations on earth.

Although verse 17 contains a new promise, much of this section simply reaffirms God's previous promises to Abraham. **Why might this have been necessary at this point? What did God indicate about Isaac's place in the covenant promises?**

7. *Genesis 22:1-19*

   *How does this story illustrate the relationship between Abraham's faith and God's promises?*

As you summarize this important lesson, ask: **What had Abraham learned through this test? What had God proven about his servant Abraham?** If you are leading a grow group, pursue the theme of redemption through sacrifice, focusing ultimately on Christ's sacrifice on the cross. **How did Jesus' death as God's only Son (see John 3:16) end this pattern of animal sacrifice? How is Abraham's story repeated in God's willingness to sacrifice his only Son for the sake of the human race?** See Romans 4; Hebrews 11:17-22; and James 2:21 for New Testament parallels. **What similarities does your group see in the two stories? What differences?**

Newcomer groups may focus on the extent of Abraham's trust in the Lord and his confidence that God would work things out. Be sensitive to your group's background and to their ability to make the connections between Christ's sacrifice and the story about Abraham and Isaac. Ask God's Spirit for guidance and discernment.

# Lesson 11

Genesis 22:20-24:9

# The Next Wife

## Introductory Notes

In this lesson your group will study Sarah's death and the search for a wife for Isaac. To introduce the lesson, you might ask what the group has learned so far about Sarah. **What was her role in Abraham's household? How was she included in the Lord's promises to Abraham?** For a New Testament reference to Sarah, you may want to read 1 Peter 3:3-6. **What can we expect will be the role of Isaac's wife and her place in the Lord's promises?**

Because the story of Isaac and Rebekah's meeting is long (from her first mention in 22:23 to their marriage in 24:67), we will cover it in three lessons.

## Optional Opening Share Question

**How would you like to be remembered?**

1. *Genesis 22:20-24*

   a. *What relationship do the people named here have to Abraham?*

   b. *Who is the only daughter mentioned?*

Apparently Abraham kept some contact with his relatives back in Mesopotamia, in the area of Haran (see a map). The family line given here contains the names of his brother Nahor's twelve sons, who would later become the heads of twelve Aramean tribes.

Be sure to note with your group the name Rebekah, the only daughter to be included in this genealogy. At this point don't jump ahead to the next lesson, where Rebekah is specifically identified as Isaac's future wife. For now, it is enough that your group sense that Rebekah may be a significant character in the story to come.

2. *Genesis 23:1-6*

   a. *What problem did Abraham face after Sarah's death?*

   b. *How did he attempt to solve this problem? What does this show about his relationship to the Hittites?*

Of all the women mentioned in the Bible, Sarah is the only one whose age and death are recorded. **Why might she have received special attention?**

Discuss with your group God's promise that Abraham and Sarah would become the "father" and "mother" of a very special line of people. **Why might Abraham not have gone back to Haran to bury Sarah? What does his desire to purchase land in Canaan for the burial say about his faith in God's promises?**

The rest of chapter 23 is an account of the legal transaction between Abraham and the Hittites for a burial ground for Sarah. As an alien and nomadic wanderer in the land of Canaan, Abraham needed permission from the Hittite community (as well as from the private landowner) to purchase a piece of land. **Why might the author of Genesis feel it necessary to include this incident in detail?** Burial grounds were extremely important to families and tribes in Abraham's culture. The author wanted to record that this exchange of money and property took place, registering the plot of land permanently as the possession of Abraham and his heirs.

**What does this interchange between Abraham and the Hittites tell us about his relationship to them?** We can note, for one thing, that Abraham was not considered part of the Hittite community; he appears not to have been on equal footing with them. (The Hittites calling him "a mighty prince" was most likely flattery and an acknowledgement of Abraham's great wealth rather than an indication that they accepted him as part of their society.) He had to receive permission from the council before purchasing a parcel of their land. **What might have been Abraham's reason for wanting to buy a burial plot of his own rather than simply using one of the Hittites' tombs, as they suggested?**

3. *Genesis 23:7-11*

   a. *What did Abraham have in mind to purchase?*
   b. *What did the owner of the field insist on?*

The city gate was the location where all business transactions requiring appropriate witnesses and community approval took place. The language the two men used is courteous and formal. Ephron's offer to "give" Abraham the plot of land (v. 9) may seem generous, but it was most likely just a polite way of beginning the bargaining procedure and not meant to be taken at face value. He was willing to part with the property—for a price, of course. **How does Abraham's behavior (v. 7) emphasize his status with the Hittites?**

Though Abraham had originally asked for just the cave, it seems that Ephron preferred to sell the entire field to him. This is not surprising, since the laws of that day required landholders to perform certain responsibilities in the community and to pay taxes on their property. If a person owned a small portion of a larger plot of land, the one who owned the larger portion of the plot would still be responsible for any duties or taxes required. Thus, if Abraham bought only the cave, Ephron would still be fully responsible as the main landowner. So Ephron was understandably eager to transfer the entire piece to Abraham.

4. *Genesis 23:12-20*

   *How did the interchange between the two men conclude?*

Since little is known of the value of the coins or weights mentioned here, we don't know for sure whether the price was high or low. Most commentaries agree, however, that Abraham probably overpaid greatly for the property. It was customary in that society for the seller to name a very high price; then the buyer would haggle and argue until they together reached a price that was satisfactory to both of them. **Why might Abraham not have tried to bargain for a better price?** Perhaps he was so eager to gain undisputed rights to this burial place that he would pay any amount. It is possible that he feared the Hittites would change their mind about letting him buy property in the land they ruled.

Ephron's comment "What is that between me and you?" is again a polite formality; he did not hesitate to take Abraham's money for the full price for the field.

Abraham's property rights are carefully spelled out in this passage so that succeeding generations would know that this specific plot of land had been properly paid for and deeded to Abraham. In fact, verses 17-18 read like an official deed.

Abraham finally buried Sarah, and it was assumed that he too—and his son Isaac—would be buried here. The cave of Machpelah had become the burial place of the "fathers," a family memorial.

5. *Genesis 24:1-4*

   a.  *How had God's favor been evident in Abraham's life, according to these verses?*

   b.  *What was Abraham concerned about?*

   c.  *How did he propose to deal with this concern?*

Use these questions to make the transition from the story of Sarah's death to the search for a wife for Isaac: **Why might this story follow that of Sarah's death? What is one of its important themes? How does it flow from the Lord's promises to Abraham and Sarah?**

The search for a suitable wife for Isaac was a final act of faith on Abraham's part. He knew that his descendants would come through Isaac, and he was anxious to find a wife suitable for such a role in God's covenant promises. **Whom did Abraham reject as possible mates for his son? Why might he have done so? Whom did he choose instead? Why?** As you discuss these questions, look again at the importance of the family line as a theme running through Genesis. **What have other marriages mentioned so far in Genesis taught us about the importance of the family line?**

67

Look, for example, at the difference between Ishmael's marriage and Isaac's coming one. **Why was Abraham so much more concerned with Isaac's wife than with Ishmael's? Whom had Ishmael married? What does this tell us about his inclusion in the family line that was to inherit God's covenant promises?**

Look also at the role that Isaac's wife would play. **What had Sarah's role been in God's covenant relationship with Abraham? In what way would Isaac's wife be a replacement for Sarah?**

As the text indicates, Abraham was very old by this time. Perhaps he feared that he would not live to see the servant's return. So he required his servant to take a binding oath. The servant put his hand under Abraham's thigh, close to his genitals, as a way of swearing this oath not only to Abraham but to all the family that would come from Abraham's seed.

6. *Genesis 24:5-6*

   a. *What concern did the servant raise?*

   b. *What solution did Abraham rule out?*

Not only did Abraham insist that the bride must come from a God-fearing family, he also emphatically stated that Isaac was not to leave the land of Canaan and go to live with his wife's family. **Why might this have been a concern for Abraham? How does this requirement demonstrate Abraham's faith in God's promises?** Abraham had been set apart, called out from his family and homeland by God. If Isaac were to return to the land of his ancestors and take up residence there, God's call to be a separate and special family—and eventually an entire nation—would come to nothing. Abraham wanted Isaac to keep his faith pure and to remain committed to the Lord and his promises. The promise of land especially was very important to Abraham; he did not want to jeopardize in any way the inheritance promised to his descendants.

7. *Genesis 24:7-9*

   a. *How did Abraham describe God?*

   b. *Why was Abraham confident of God's help in this matter?*

   c. *Under what condition would the servant be released from his oath?*

These are the last recorded words of Abraham. Use them to summarize his life so far. **How do they contrast with his first recorded words (Gen. 15:2-3, 8)? What might account for the difference in tone and content?**

Ask your group how Abraham's words might provide a transition into the next part of the story. **What are we led to expect? What sort of woman would be the object of the servant's search? How urgent was his task?** Use these questions not only to summarize the passage for today but also to anticipate the next lesson.

# Lesson 12
Genesis 24:10-54

# Answered Prayer

## Introductory Notes

Since this lesson continues the story of lesson 11, you may want to introduce it by summarizing Genesis 24:1-9. Ask these questions to make the transition: **In what situation did Abraham find himself? About what was he concerned? Of what was he confident? How did he express that confidence? What kind of wife did he want for Isaac? Why? Why did Abraham send a servant back to his relatives?** Since the story of Isaac and Rebekah will not be concluded in this lesson, be prepared to leave the end of your discussion somewhat open-ended.

## Optional Opening Share Question

**Have you ever gone on a blind date?**

1. *Genesis 24:10-11*

   *How did the servant plan to meet the girl he was looking for?*

   Though most of Abraham's journeys are described only briefly, the one undertaken by his servant is full of specific details. (Compare it with Gen. 12:1-6, for example.) **Why might so much detail have been included here? What is important about the details mentioned? What do they tell us about the servant's obedience to Abraham's more general instructions?**

   According to this account, the servant timed his approach to Nahor so that he would arrive in the evening about the time the women of the city went to the well to draw water. **What advantage did this give him?**

2. *Genesis 24:12-14*

   a. *On what basis did the servant ask for God's help?*

   b. *What did he ask of the Lord?*

   Aside from Abraham's conversations with God, this is the first recorded prayer in the Bible. **What does it tell us about prayer itself? What kind of language did the servant use in his prayer? Is it formal and impersonal? What does it assume about God? How specific are the requests?** Help your group to see that this prayer is relational, person to Person. **How did the servant address God?** The phrase "God of my master Abraham" is prominent in this prayer. **What does it tell us about the servant's relationship to God?**

Also help your group to see that this prayer is not a request for a miracle; it is a very ordinary and practical request. **What kind of person would offer to water the servant's camels? What did that have to do with the kind of woman the servant was looking for?** The servant knew that such a woman would be generous and thoughtful, since she would have to draw much more water than usual to satisfy the camels' thirst after their long journey.

The servant asks God for two things: that God show him the girl who is right for Isaac and that God continue to bless his master, Abraham.

3. *Genesis 24:15-16*

   a. *How did the Lord answer the servant's prayer?*

   b. *In what ways was Rebekah qualified to be Isaac's wife?*

The remarkable thing about this part of the story is the immediacy of God's reply to the servant's prayer. **How quickly did God answer?** "Before he had finished praying"! **What details are given here about Rebekah? How is each one important? How did she fit the general guidelines Abraham had given his servant? How does this description go even beyond those guidelines?**

4. *Genesis 24:17-21*

   a. *How did Rebekah respond to the servant's request for water?*

   b. *How did the servant respond to Rebekah? What was he looking for?*

The Old Testament idea of beauty included not only looks but also the ability to perform everyday work well. **How was Rebekah beautiful in this way as well? What do her actions reveal about her?**

**How sensitive was Rebekah to the needs of the servant and his animals?** Not only did Rebekah offer to draw water for the camels, but she did not stop working until the camels' thirst had been completely satisfied. She went far beyond the servant's request for "a little drink of water." **What did this tell the servant about her character?**

5. *Genesis 24:22-27*

   a. *What more did the servant ask of Rebekah?*

   b. *How did her response answer the servant's prayer?*

   c. *What did the servant learn about the Lord's character as a result?*

The gifts that Abraham's servant gave to the girl seem quite lavish. **Did he give them to her before or after he learned who she was? What might have been his reasons for giving her these gifts?** The gold nose ring and bracelets were given in part as thanks for her efforts in watering the camels. But they also indicated that the servant had more than a passing interest in her; they were a sign of honor and respect as well.

**Why was the servant overjoyed at Rebekah's response (v. 24)? How was her answer related to the genealogy in Genesis 22:20-24?** The servant's prayer (see vv. 13-14, 21) had been answered. Not only did the girl have a character worthy of Isaac, but she was also from the right family. **How did the servant respond to the Lord's speedy answer? Who was the focus of the prayer? How was it an appropriate conclusion to the servant's earlier requests? In what way had this journey been an act of faith for both Abraham and his servant? How did this act of worship relate to the others we have seen in the story of Abraham?** Use these questions to discuss the servant's prayer of thanksgiving.

6. *Genesis 24:28-33*

   a. *Whom did the girl run and tell?*

   b. *What was the family's response?*

Even the small, commonplace details are recorded here to indicate their importance in the servant's analysis of Rebekah.

It is not clear why Laban, her brother, plays such an important role here while her father is not mentioned; perhaps her father was ill or very old (note also that she ran to "her mother's household"). Or, as was common in that culture, Laban as eldest son may have been granted the power of authority in the household. At any rate, Laban would also play an important part in later chapters, especially in his dealings with Jacob, Isaac's son. Although he is later shown to be a greedy, manipulative man, his behavior here is consistent with the customs of hospitality of that time. **Might the family have guessed already who the servant was? What had Rebekah heard the servant say in his prayer (v. 27)? How had he identified himself?**

7. *Genesis 24:34-41*

   a. *How did the servant summarize God's blessings to Abraham and Sarah?*

   b. *According to the servant, what command had Abraham given him?*

   c. *How did the servant identify Abraham's God?*

   d. *How do the servant's words compare with Abraham's instructions (vv. 6-9)?*

The servant formally introduced himself and gave the details of his mission, explaining his interest in Rebekah. As he did so, he told the history of the Lord's hand in his journey, emphasizing that the Lord had prospered him and his master. **What details did the servant highlight in his account? Why might he have done so? For example, what reasons may he have had** for dwelling on Abraham's wealth and the fact that Isaac was the sole heir? Apparently the servant wanted to make Isaac's offer of marriage more attractive to Rebekah and her family. He did not stress Abraham's insistence that the prospective bride leave her family and travel back to Canaan. Perhaps he felt that could wait for later negotiations.

8. *Genesis 24:42-51*

    a. *How did the servant explain his belief that Rebekah was the woman for Isaac?*

    b. *What indicates that the servant was absolutely sure of the correctness of his choice?*

    c. *How did Laban and Bethuel respond? Why do you think they responded this way?*

Throughout this story the servant consistently placed himself in the background, emphasizing instead his master Abraham and the God of Abraham. In the process, he did a superb job of making his offer as attractive as possible, hoping that Rebekah's family would say yes. **Why might the servant have stressed "kindness" and "faithfulness" (v. 49)? Where else had the servant mentioned these words? (See vv. 12 and 27.) In what way could Laban and his family take part in God's faithfulness to Abraham?**

Spend some time discussing Laban and Bethuel's response. **What are its most important elements? What do these men affirm about the Lord? What are they saying yes to? What had convinced them?**

9. *Genesis 24:52-54*

    *What did the servant do after the negotiations were finished?*

At last the servant could relax from the strain of his serious duties (see v. 33). He brought out the gifts for Isaac's new bride and for her family, then celebrated the accomplishment of his mission with food and drink. His oath had been fulfilled.

As you summarize what you've learned in this lesson, ask your group how the Lord had demonstrated faithfulness to Abraham and his servant. **What relationship was there between the servant's words and actions and the Lord's working? What does this tell us about the way the Lord works on behalf of his people? About prayer?** Also reflect on the length of the story. **Why might this story be so long and detailed? What does this tell us about the story's importance?**

Remember, the story is not finished. Rebekah had not yet left her father's house. **What was left for the servant to do? What obstacles might lie in the way?**

# Lesson 13

Genesis 24:54-25:11

# Beginning and Ending

## Introductory Notes

Once again, summarize the story of Isaac and Rebekah to refresh your group's memory of what you've studied so far. **What had the servant experienced to this point? How successful was his mission? What did he yet have to accomplish?**

## Optional Opening Share Question

**Have you ever moved far away from your family?**

1. *Genesis 24:54-61*
   a. *Why might the servant have wished to leave immediately?*
   b. *How was the outcome of this incident a further answer to the servant's prayer?*
   c. *How is the blessing given to Rebekah similar to God's blessing on Abraham?*

Apparently the servant's proposal to leave so soon was highly irregular in this very hospitable culture. Courtesy called for the host to entertain eminent guests ten days or more, and Laban urged his guest to stay. But the servant was probably eager to leave while he still had the high esteem of the family. He may still have been unsure about the family's willingness to let Rebekah go.

When the servant persisted in his request to leave, Laban checked with Rebekah to find out whether she was willing to make this journey. **How does this coincide with Abraham's words (see Gen. 24:8)? What was Rebekah's response? Whom did she take with her on the journey?** Rebekah's response indicates the depth of her character. She became part of Abraham's family of faith by her willingness to respond immediately to God's call to leave home and country, just as Abraham had done earlier. **What does this indicate also about her belief in Abraham's God?**

The blessing Rebekah received is an ancient farewell blessing typical of that culture. As you discuss the similarities and differences between this blessing and God's blessings to Abraham, ask: **What does this blessing suggest about the beliefs Rebekah was coming from?**

2. *Genesis 24:62-67*

    a. *How did Rebekah and Isaac meet?*

    b. *What had the servant "done" (v. 66)?*

    c. *What do we learn about Isaac here? About Isaac and Rebekah's wedding?*

The story of Isaac and Rebekah has brought us some "firsts"—the first recorded prayer in the Bible, and now the first marriage mentioned in the Bible (and the first time the word *love* is used for the relationship between a man and woman).

Verses 62-67 contain some ambiguities: the Hebrew word translated "meditate" (v. 63), for example, is of uncertain meaning. In addition, it is not clear why Rebekah felt it necessary to veil herself before meeting Isaac, since women of that time did not ordinarily veil themselves. And the reference to Sarah (v. 67) is also unclear; it may imply that Rebekah took over Sarah's role as mistress of the house.

Note that the servant refers to Isaac as "my master" (v. 65). **What does this tell us about Isaac's status over Abraham's estate?** It is possible that Abraham may have been dead by this time, judging from the tone of his words to his servant earlier (Gen. 24:1-8). In that case, the sequence of events recorded here (particularly in chapter 25, which tells of Abraham's marriage to Keturah and his later death) is not necessarily chronological. At any rate, the family leadership had clearly passed on to Isaac and Rebekah.

This is the conclusion of the story of the search for Isaac's wife. Summarize the story with some of the following questions: **What is the most important theme or idea in the story? Why might this story have been included in the Bible? What does it tell us about Abraham's relationship to the Lord? His relationship to Isaac? What might we expect from the life of Isaac and Rebekah? What does this story teach us about prayer?**

3. *Genesis 25:1-4*

    *What do these verses tell us about the fulfillment of God's promises to Abraham?*

This section is concerned with both the past and the future. As noted above, it may not follow chronologically from chapter 24. Abraham may have died before Isaac's marriage to Rebekah. Though the placement of this chapter makes it sound as though Abraham took Keturah as his wife after Sarah's death, it is possible that she was a second wife (or concubine, see 1 Chron. 1:32) during the time that Sarah was alive. Scholars suggest this because it seems unlikely that Abraham would have sent Keturah's sons away before they had reached the age of forty (the usual age for marriage at that time). Abraham lived only thirty-eight years after Sarah's death, so even his oldest sons by Keturah would not have been forty years old by that time, had they been born after Sarah's death. Perhaps the account mentions Keturah here only to conclude Abraham's history and the list of his descendants.

The names listed here are those of Arab tribes, similar to the names connected with Ishmael's sons. Again, this emphasizes the common family root shared by the people of the Middle East. Although his descendants are listed, they are excluded from the line of God's people (though they appear frequently in later Israelite history).

4.  *Genesis 25:5-6*

    *How did Abraham treat Isaac in comparison to the rest of his sons?*

**Why did Abraham send away the sons he had fathered through Keturah?** The same principle that sent Ishmael away into the desert applied to these sons as well. Isaac was the son of promise, and Abraham was determined that he would be treated as the single heir, the one who would continue the family line and receive the covenant promises. **How does this reflect Abraham's faith in God's promises?**

Abraham was generous with all of his sons, making sure they were well provided for before they left his household. Note that Ishmael received special treatment, having received a blessing from God as well. However, Isaac was clearly the sole heir of Abraham's material goods and the covenant promises given to Abraham and his descendants.

5.  *Genesis 25:7-11*

    a.  *What does this passage tell us about Abraham?*

    b.  *How is his life summarized?*

Remind your group that in those days old age was considered a sign of God's blessing, an indication of a righteous life. Abraham's death ends the account of Terah begun in Genesis 11:27. Note that Abraham died one hundred years after he had left his father's house in Haran.

**Who attended Abraham's burial? Where was Abraham buried?** Both Ishmael and Isaac came to bury their father, another indication that Ishmael held a special place in Abraham's family as the oldest son.

6.  *Genesis 11:27-25:18*

    a.  *What kind of God had the God of Abraham proved himself to be?*

    b.  *In what ways did Abraham and Sarah live a life of faith?*

    c.  *How had God's plan for the world unfolded through Abraham and Sarah?*

Use these summary questions to look together at Abraham and Sarah's role in the Lord's plan for saving the world. Refer to Genesis 3, which sheds light on the presence of sin and death in the world. **What promises had God** made to Abraham? **In light of Genesis 1-3, what do those promises mean for humankind?** Help your group to see that the story of Abraham also looks forward. **How do these promises predict the future of the world? Of Abraham's and Sarah's descendants?**

# Evaluation Questionnaire

## DISCOVER GENESIS: ABRAHAM AND SARAH

As you complete this study, please fill out this questionnaire to help us evaluate the effectiveness of our materials. Please be candid. Thank you.

1. Was this a home group ___ or a church-based ___ program? What church?

2. Was the study used for
   ___ a community evangelism group?
   ___ a community grow group?
   ___ a church Bible study group?

3. How would you rate the materials?

   Study Guide
   ___ excellent ___ very good ___ good ___ fair ___ poor

   Leader Guide
   ___ excellent ___ very good ___ good ___ fair ___ poor

4. What were the strengths?

5. What were the weaknesses?

6. What would you suggest to improve the material?

7. In general, what was the experience of your group?

Your name (optional) _____

Address _____

8.  Other comments:

(Please fold, tape, stamp, and mail. Thank you.)

Faith Alive
2850 Kalamazoo Ave. SE
Grand Rapids, MI 49560-0300